Robert Westall

THE MACHINE GUNNERS

adapted for the stage by
Ali Taylor

NICK HERN BOOKS

London

www.nickhernbooks.co.uk

A Nick Hern Book

This stage adaptation of *The Machine Gunners* first published in Great Britain as a paperback original in 2012 by Nick Hern Books Limited, The Glasshouse, 49a Goldhawk Road, London W12 8QP

The Machine Gunners (novel) copyright © 1975 Robert Westall
The Machine Gunners (play) copyright © 2012 Ali Taylor

Ali Taylor and Robert Westall have asserted their right to be identified as the authors of this work

Front and back cover images: the original cast of the 2011 Polka Theatre production of *The Machine Gunners*; photograph by Robert Workman
Cover design by Ned Hoste, 2H

Typeset by Nick Hern Books, London
Printed and bound in Great Britain by Mimeo Ltd, Cambridgeshire PE29 6XX

A CIP catalogue record for this book is available from the British Library

ISBN 978 1 84842 314 5

Production Notes
by Ali Taylor, adapter of *The Machine Gunners*

This adaptation was commissioned by Polka Theatre for a production in spring 2011. These notes draw on that first staging and the creative ideas behind it.

Adapting the Novel

Between the ages of about ten and twelve, *The Machine Gunners* was my favourite book. I can remember reading it over and over, loving the mix of adventure, camaraderie and danger. When Polka asked me to write an adaptation I was thrilled but also a bit worried: would Robert Westall's story be as good as I remembered it? Would it have the same magic? Would it feel dated? I went on to Amazon, bought a copy and was happy to find the story was just as gripping twenty years on.

From the first page, you're immersed in Chas McGill's world, an alien place of shelters and rationing, air raids and bomb damage. But as unfamiliar as it is to a modern reader, it's also a recognisable world full of sausage and chips, school lessons and playground bullies. It feels incredibly real.

As you're introduced to the characters in the fictional town of Garmouth, you quickly discover this is no jingoistic account of how brave Blighty overcame the Hun. Westall tells it like it is. Nightly bombing raids have shaken the fabric of the society. The adults are shown as exhausted shells of themselves who struggle to maintain a normal family life while the world collapses around them. The children, without parental control, are largely allowed to roam free – something alien to most children today. For them, the bombed-out houses are a playground, a place to explore and – importantly for Chas – to collect debris as souvenirs.

It's the children who are the centre of the story. Westall's portrayal of Chas and his gang is refreshingly unsentimental. Chas, in particular, is a wonderful character: devilish, brave, conniving and tough. Once he finds the machine gun he single-mindedly searches for ways to keep it, even if it means fighting dirty, manipulating his friends and lying to his dad. His motley gang of outsiders are dragged along in his wake: Cem the joker, Audrey the tomboy, Nicky the bullied posh boy and Clogger the brooding hard man from Glasgow.

In Nicky's garden they build Fortress Caparetto – ostensibly to have a base for shooting down German planes, but more to give them a place to call their own and provide the supportive relationships their families can no longer offer.

Against a backdrop of death and destruction, we watch the gang come of age. The way they care for Nicky after his house is bombed never fails to be touching. And the generosity shown towards captured pilot Rudi – as they learn that German soldiers are normal people too – demonstrates the depth of their humanity.

The Machine Gunners may be written for children, but it has themes that are as profound and as challenging as in any adult fiction. It forces young readers to confront difficult subjects: grief, violence, relationships with parents and personal responsibility. Perhaps what makes the book so special is that it tackles these subjects completely straight and refuses to ever talk down to its audience.

When it came to adapting the novel, I was certain that my script should remain true to the spirit and tone of Westall's book. I would keep its realism, honesty and complexity, as well as retain the rebelliousness and fun.

Stylistically, I also wanted to put my own stamp on it. I love plays that are theatrical and use all the possibilities of the stage. There seemed no reason why, if it was played truthfully, scenes couldn't be a mix of naturalism and high theatricality. Amid scenes of kitchen-sink naturalism, I have Chas breaking the fourth wall to speak directly to the audience. I gave his monologues a poetic edge. And I suggested moments for stylised movement. In future productions I would encourage people to be as theatrical and as imaginative in staging as their minds (and budgets) allow them, while playing it emotionally and psychologically true.

Just as important as capturing the emotional story was making the play exciting. *The Machine Gunners* is a thriller and I was determined that we kept the young audience on the edge of their seats. I kept the scenes short and punchy and the production team used lighting and sound to make scene changes fast and fluid. Enormous subwoofers under the seating made the audience physically feel the boom and rumble of an air raid.

Much of the excitement, in the early part of the story, comes from Chas's attempts to keep one step ahead of the pursuing police. But in the second half, even more tension is created by the imminent threat of German invasion.

Today, it's easy to forget that an Allied victory against the Nazis was, by no means, a sure thing. Decades of film and television has made victory seem inevitable, but the outcome was very uncertain in 1940/41. People genuinely believed Hitler would successfully invade Britain and they had good reason to believe so. Belgium, Poland and France had all fallen and Britain was next. People were justifiably terrified. In his story, Westall shows clearly what effect fear has on both adults and children alike. The Partons flee to the countryside, rumours spread around town, and in the climax of the book, the children come within a hair's breadth of mowing down their families in machine-gun fire. It's crucial that in future productions the cast plays the stakes high and real.

Some aspects of the adaptation were tricky. There are dozens of characters in the book and from the outset I was told I had six actors. As this is a story filled with more than twenty characters it meant that, even after doubling, some of the supporting roles would have to go. But who? Minor characters like Carrot Juice fell by the wayside as did Big John. Mrs Spalding appeared in a draft briefly for comedy value but had to be lost. I conflated the characters of Fatty Hardy and Sergeant Green. And I changed the Polish soldiers to the Home Guard for simplicity.

The portrayal of violence proved particularly challenging. There are two bloody and brutal fights in the book. While Westall's prose is tough, reading allows children to imagine a level of violence that is acceptable to them. On stage it is different. Seeing two adult actors hitting each other is much more literal, and potentially upsetting. We chose to be more suggestive, having Chas narrate the fights, while the actors played out a piece of stylised, choreographed movement. This worked well and it's an option for future productions.

In the script, I began the play with a description of an air raid. Director Adam Penford cleverly interpreted this stage direction by projecting film footage of a German bombing raid onto white sheets on Mrs McGill's washing line. I'm aware that film footage may not be available or affordable, so I'd encourage directors to find their own imaginative solutions.

Design

In creating a fast and dynamic production, we knew we needed an all-purpose, non-literal set. With multiple locations and dozens of quick scene changes, simplicity was key. Designer Simon Kenny created a set that imagined a bomb had fallen on the roof of the theatre, bringing down one of the arch supports and scattering the stage with debris. With Chas acting as a storyteller, he and the gang created the world as he described it, using the debris to suggest different locations. So dining chairs became school chairs and sandbags became the walls of the fortress. Simon also added in a variety of levels and playing areas with traps, poles and moveable sections.

Costumes were in period style but simple – a hat, jacket and/or pair of glasses to indicate a change of character – to allow quick changes.

Language

The story feels very rooted in the north-east and it portrays a specific working-class community. Ideally, future productions would be true to the language and rhythms of the area. But, in saying that, if mastering the accents is too tricky then companies should use equivalent words or expressions. I think it's more important that the characters feel real than risk losing an audience's belief in the world of the play.

If you'd like to give the accents a go, here's a glossary of slang and German:

Cannet	Can't
Divnt	Don't
Shacker	Coward
Neb	Nose
Hellish	Brilliant
Bairn	Child
Gadgies	Old men
Cackle	Foolish chatter
Lug	Ear
Quislings	Collaborators
Champion	Excellent
Ye knar	You know
Greetin'	Crying
Ye ken	You know
Glasgae kiss	Head butt
Nippin' ma heed	Annoying me
Ja/Nein	Yes/No
Dummkopf	Idiot
Hände hoch	Hands up
Bitte	Please
Mein Got	My God
Wo bin ich?	Where am I?
Freund	Friend
Bog	Toilet
Kameraden	Comrades

Casting

This version of *The Machine Gunners* was written for a company of six actors but it can accommodate many more according to the needs of each production.

The roles can be doubled and trebled up as follows:

ACTOR 1	Chas McGill
ACTOR 2	Cem Jones / Warden
ACTOR 3	Audrey Parton / Mrs Maggie McGill
ACTOR 4	Benjamin 'Nicky' Nichol / Fatty Hardy / Warden
ACTOR 5	Clogger Duncan / Mr Jack McGill
ACTOR 6	Rudi Gerlath / Stan Liddell / Boddser Brown

With a large cast, there's scope for creating the world of Garmouth more fully than we were able in the original production. There's the potential for showing, for example, the townspeople that Chas passes on the way to Chirton, the pupils in the playground, the wardens and Home Guard.

Thanks

Thanks to Jon Lloyd and everyone at Polka Theatre for the energy, commitment and enthusiasm given to the production. And special thanks to Adam Penford for the dedication and intelligence he gave to the script. I'd also like to thank Charlotte Knight and the Knight Hall Agency, as well as Justine Grimley and the cast for helping with Geordie slang.

This adaptation of *The Machine Gunners* was first performed at Polka Theatre, London, on 11 February 2011. The cast was as follows:

CHAS McGILL	Michael Imerson
CEM JONES / WARDEN	Scott Turnbull
AUDREY PARTON /	Claire Sundin
MRS MAGGIE McGILL	
BENJAMIN 'NICKY' NICHOL /	Chris Coxon
FATTY HARDY / WARDEN	
CLOGGER DUNCAN /	David Kirkbride
MR JACK McGILL	
RUDI GERLATH / STAN LIDDELL /	Matthew Brown
BODDSER BROWN	

Director	Adam Penford
Assistant Director	Richard Fitch
Designer	Simon Kenny
Lighting Designer	Emma Chapman
Sound Designer	Tom Gibbons
Assistant Sound Designer	Max Perryment

Film footage was supplied by the Imperial War Museum, London.

THE MACHINE GUNNERS

Adapted for the stage by Ali Taylor

From the book by Robert Westall

Characters

FATTY HARDY
CHAS McGILL
MR JACK McGILL
MRS MAGGIE McGILL
CEM JONES
BODDSER BROWN
AUDREY PARTON
STAN LIDDELL
CLOGGER DUNCAN
BENJAMIN 'NICKY' NICHOL
RUDI GERLATH
FIRST WARDEN
SECOND WARDEN

Note on Text

(*T/A*.) 'To Audience'; indicates where a section of direct address should begin

/ indicates an interruption

– indicates where a sentence is stopped by the speaker

… indicates where a thought drifts away

The play is written for a minimum of six actors, who can double and treble the roles. For suggested doubling and casting notes, please see page x.

Style

The intention is that the action should be fluid, with scenes melting into one another. Rather than number the scenes, I've used stars (***) so that there is less of a sense of scenes being broken up.

ACT ONE

1 November 1940. Midnight.

Garmouth, a town in north-east England.

A gramophone is playing a popular song from the Blitz.

We hear the low drone of German aeroplanes approaching and the thump of bombs dropping. As the rumble builds, so the record skips, and the song begins jumping and crackling. Eventually, the song is drowned out by the thunderous sound of the air raid.

We now hear the air-raid sirens and see beams of light shine into the night sky. Tracer bullets spit up from the ground.

Two Heinkel bombers thunder over the town, weaving their way through the searchlights and gunfire.

They discharge their bombs. Factories, churches and terraced houses explode. The town is engulfed in flames and smoke. It glows.

An RAF Spitfire appears. The rattle of gunfire. It peppers the Heinkel bombers with bullets. One Heinkel splutters before going into a nosedive. We hear the whine as it plummets to earth, crashing in a ball of flames.

* * *

2 November 1940. Morning.

Through the smoke and fog, policeman FATTY HARDY *patrols the streets, blowing a whistle.*

FATTY. All clear! All clear!

* * *

CHAS McGILL *emerges out of an air-raid shelter at the bottom of his garden.*

CHAS (*T/A*). My name is Chas McGill. And this is me shelter at the bottom of me garden…

Concurrently, we see JACK, *dressed in his warden's uniform, sat at the kitchen table. He is exhausted.* MAGGIE, *dressed in a floral-print dress and pinny, is serving breakfast.* JACK *makes a sausage sandwich.*

CHAS *heads towards the kitchen.*

…The garden of me house at number nineteen Marston Street, Garmouth

The north-east of England

Overlooking the North Sea.

That's me mam and that's me dad.

MAGGIE. Come on, Chas! It's eight o'clock. You're late for school!

JACK. Aye, c'mon, lad. Yer mam's made us sausage butties.

CHAS. Hellish!

(*T/A.*) Rations mean we never get sausage for breakfast.

MAGGIE. It's yer lucky day, Chas.

Get a move on. I won't have yer late again.

CHAS. But I haven't got school till ha' past ten.

CHAS *begins putting on his school uniform.*

MAGGIE. Half ten. How so?

CHAS. Air raid went past midnight, didn't it. It's a new rule.

JACK. Don't yer believe it, Mam.

CHAS. Honestly! It's a new rule.

JACK. Suppose we'll have to take yer word. You're no liar, are yer, Chassy?

CHAS. No, Dad.

MAGGIE. Eat them before they get cold.

JACK *eats his sandwich*.

CHAS (*T/A*). Dad works in a factory in the day and as a warden at night. Mam stays at home and keeps our house cleaner than the Haughtons at number twenty-one.

JACK. Terrible raid last night.

MAGGIE. I got no sleep.

I thought it was never gonna end. I could swear me and Chas were gonna get buried alive in that shelter.

JACK. Ye hear about that lass in the greengrocer's?

MAGGIE. Not the ginger-haired one?

JACK. Aye. Direct hit. We found half of her in the front garden and half right across the house.

MAGGIE *holds her hand over her mouth*.

MAGGIE (*whispers*). Jack, why say that in front of the bairn?

That's awful!

JACK. He has to learn some time that the world isn't all warm baths and comics.

CHAS. Was it that dive-bomber that done it?

JACK. No, a Heinkel I'm sure. The RAF lads shot him down and he crashed right onto the old laundry at Chirton. With a full bomb load. I felt the heat on me face a mile away.

CHAS. Is anything left of it?

JACK. Not the laundry.

CHAS. The bomber, I mean.

JACK. Bits I suppose.

MAGGIE. Don't be getting ideas, Chas McGill.

CHAS. Aw, Mam. Let us have a look.

JACK. There won't be nowt but bricks.

CHAS. Mam?

MAGGIE. No.

JACK. Go on, let him.

CHAS. Yeah, go on, let us.

MAGGIE. I don't like yer playing round bombsites.

CHAS. I'll be fine.

MAGGIE. Okay. But be careful. And mind, if you bring back souvenirs, they'll go in the greenhouse. I won't have any of yer junk in here.

And remember, I want you in school by quarter past ten… at the latest.

CHAS. Thanks, Mam!

* * *

Streets of Garmouth.

CHAS *grabs his satchel and runs towards the old laundry. His route is littered with piles of debris from the recent air raid.*

CHAS (*T/A*). Out the door, down me street and on me way to Chirton.

I dodge past the piles of bricks, plaster, tiles and beams.

I weave past the wardens shovelling

Women sweeping

Little kids watching

All making Marston Street back to normal.

Enter CEM.

At the junction, I'm joined by me best mate Cem.

CEM *does a little bow of greeting to* CHAS. CHAS *smiles*.

CEM. Cemetery Jones at your service.

CHAS (*T/A*). His dad's the local undertaker.

CEM *pretends to be a zombie. The boys continue on their journey.*

For the rest of Garmouth, you'll have to use your imagination for what it looks like.

CEM. It divnt look like it used to look like.

CHAS (*T/A*). Three months of German bombs have seen to that.

(*Indicates a pile of rubble.*) That used to be the church.

CEM (*indicates a pile of rubble*). That used to be the butcher's.

CHAS (*indicates a pile of rubble*). And that was me mam's hairdresser.

CEM. The Town Hall's still standing.

CHAS. And our school.

CEM. I know, man. Don't remind me!

CHAS (*prays*). Please God or Hitler or whoever send down a bomb on Garmouth High School.

CEM (*joins in*). I'll eat me greens.

CHAS (*joins in*). And I'll help auld gadgies cross the road.

The boys laugh.

CEM. We collecting souvenirs today then, Chas?

CHAS. Aye, you not heard? A Heinkel's crashed on top of the laundry in Chirton.

CEM. No way! They'll be loads then!

CHAS. Tonnes!

CEM. To add to yer collection!

CHAS (*T/A*). Aye, me collection:

> Eleven incendiary bomb fins, twenty-six spent bullets,
> eighteen pieces of shrapnel, fifty empty cartridge cases.

> And a tail fin from an SC50.

CEM. The second-best collection of war souvenirs in
Garmouth.

> *Lights up on* BODDSER *standing to one side in his school
> uniform, looking smug.*

CHAS (*T/A*). Only Boddser Brown's got anything better.

CEM. How much do I *hate* him!

CHAS. He's a right stupid chockhead.

CEM. And looks like a frog with constipation!

> BODDSER *responds, perhaps cracking his knuckles or
> smirking at them.*

CHAS (*T/A*). You'll meet him later.

> *Lights down on* BODDSER.

CEM. We've got be quick, Chas. Only an hour till school starts.

* * *

> *The grounds of the laundry. West Chirton.*

CHAS (*T/A*). We arrive at the laundry half an hour later.

CEM. Is this it?

> There's nowt left.

CHAS (*T/A*). He's right. It's a just a ruin of broken walls,
collapsed concrete

> And piles and piles of bricks and girders

> All twisted, bent and broken.

> The whole place stinks of oil and dust.

Enter AUDREY.

AUDREY. What are youse two up to?

CEM. Oh no!

CHAS. Audrey Parton!

AUDREY. That's me name. Don't waste it.

CHAS (*T/A*). Audrey's the bossiest girl in our class. She's too much of a boy to be liked by the girls and too much of a nosy parker to be liked by us.

AUDREY. Alright, Charles? Cyril?

CEM. God! Me name's Cem. Cem. C – E – M.

AUDREY. Sorry, Cyril. I am forgetful.

CHAS. Yer not got any little dolls to play with?

AUDREY. Just youse two. What are you up to?

CEM. None of your business. Keep yer neb out.

AUDREY. You're a long way from school.

And why you walking in the wrong direction?

CEM. Like I say, none of yours. Do one.

AUDREY. Only if you let me join in.

CHAS *and* CEM *look at each other.*

CEM (*to* CHAS). Please – no, Chas.

CHAS. She might be useful. Them muscles of hers.

CEM. Your call. But don't blame me if she covers yer in make-up.

CHAS (*reluctant, to* AUDREY). Okay then. Yer can come with us. But only for ten minutes. And no talking about girl stuff.

AUDREY. Thank you.

CHAS. We're combing the whole place for souvenirs. I want every inch searched. Quick smart.

They split up and begin searching the area.

Don't bother looking in the obvious places. You've got to look where no one else does. Behind bins and under bushes.

CEM *holds up a piece of metal.*

AUDREY. It all looks like rubble to me.

CEM. Funny that. With this being a bombsite.

This any good, Chas?

CHAS. No, I've got eleven of those already.

CEM. This?

CHAS. No. That's a tin can.

AUDREY *holds up a piece of brick.*

AUDREY. This?

CHAS. And that's just a brick.

They look. CHAS *finds a piece of propeller from the Heinkel engine.*

Wait, stop. Look at this. Bit of propeller from the Heinkel's engine. Yer knar what this means? We must be close to where it landed. Pass me bag to put this in to.

FATTY *(off).* Hey. What do you think you're doing?

CEM. Oh no!

AUDREY. Fatty Hardy!

CHAS *passes the propeller to* CEM, *who passes it to* AUDREY, *who hides it behind her back. Enter* FATTY HARDY.

CHAS *(T/A, sarcastic).* Fatty Hardy. Garmouth's answer to Sherlock Holmes. Except nowt near as clever and always pestering folk like us.

FATTY. Your mams know you're out?

CHAS. Aye.

FATTY. They let you play on crash sites?

AUDREY. No –

CEM. Aye. All the time.

FATTY. There could be unexploded bombs all over here. It's far too dangerous for little kids like you.

CHAS. We're not little!

FATTY. Come on, get lost. Yer must have homes to go to.

CHAS. Not for long.

FATTY. Meaning what?

CHAS. Fatty... I mean, Constable Hardy, we've got a deep hole in our back garden... and me mam's heard ticking from it.

FATTY. A likely story.

CHAS. True, sir. I was sent out to find yer.

FATTY. Do yer think I'm stupid, lad?

CHAS. Aye, I mean no, sir.

FATTY. Where do yer live?

CHAS. It's a *hundred* and nineteen Marston Street.

CEM. Yer better go quick.

CHAS. We'll keep watch round here. Make sure little kids don't touch anything.

FATTY. I'll have a look, but if you're lying to me...

CHAS. No, sir.

FATTY. ... then I'll have you up for wasting police time.

AUDREY. Quickly, Constable Hardy.

FATTY. I don't want to see youse here when I get back. You should be in school. Idle kids make trouble.

FATTY *moves to leave.* CHAS *turns to* CEM *to check he still has the propeller.* AUDREY *shows it to* CHAS. *She drops it.*

Wait up, there is no a hundred and nineteen Marston Street.

What's that?

The children freeze. They look to each other.

CHAS. Run!

CEM. Run?

AUDREY. Run!

* * *

West Chirton Wood. Late afternoon.

The children have just stopped running. They're out of breath. They stop and look around. It's dark, damp, unfamiliar.

AUDREY. Wait, stop, I'm right knackered.

CEM. Where's this, Chas?

CHAS. West Chirton Wood. You've not been here?

AUDREY. No. Mam says I'm only to go a mile distance from the house and no more. This is miles and –

I don't know about this.

It's dark under these trees. And right spooky. And we're missing school.

CEM. Stinks.

CHAS. Grown-ups dump all sorts in here.

CEM. Smells like petrol.

AUDREY. Must be from fireworks.

CHAS *is on to something. He's like a bloodhound that's found a scent.*

CHAS. No. No one dumps petrol. It's too expensive.

It's something else.

CEM. Aw, am getting stung by nettles, man.

AUDREY. And I've ripped me stockings, Chas. Mam's gonna kill us.

CHAS. There's something about this place that's –

CHAS *starts investigating.* AUDREY *fixes her socks.*

AUDREY. If all this is one of yer tricks, Chas McGill. I'm not doing any dirty things with youse two, so you needn't think I am. I divnt mind kissing but no more.

CEM. Euurgh. No thank you.

CHAS. Sssh.

CHAS *motions for them to duck. They duck.*

CEM. What is it, Chas?

AUDREY. Fatty Hardy I bet. I knew he'd catch us.

CHAS *points towards the branches of the trees. He climbs up and pulls back tree branches to reveal the tail fin of a German bomber – with a swastika on the side.*

CHAS. No. Look.

AUDREY. What is it?

CHAS. A rudder, I'd say.

CEM *and* AUDREY *scramble up behind* CHAS.

CEM. Of the Heinkel?

CHAS. Aye, help us move it.

They push the rudder out of the way. They see the body of the crashed Heinkel bomber.

There it is.

CHAS *approaches the cockpit. He is about to open it –*

AUDREY. Don't!

CHAS *hesitates. Then opens the lid. A dead pilot flops over, dangling out of his seat. CHAS steps back, shocked. AUDREY and CEM cry out/scream.*

Is he – ?

CHAS. Aye. Very.

CEM *climbs to the top. He pulls his jumper over his mouth and wafts away the flies. He pushes the pilot's stiff arm. It swings.*

CEM. One for me dad I suppose.

AUDREY. He don't bury Germans.

CEM. Does so. He's got coffins full of bits of them at the cemetery.

CHAS. He really smells.

AUDREY. Poor man. He's got a nice face. He's a long way from home.

CEM. So am I. And honest I divnt like it.

CHAS. You shouldn't look. It's not something for girls.

AUDREY. Give over. You're the one that's gone green.

I wonder what his name was.

CHAS *spots something*

CEM. Doesn't matter. He's a Nazi. Only good Nazi's a dead Nazi.

AUDREY. You're heartless, Cemetery Jones.

CEM. Chas? What's up?

CHAS *pulls another branch away to reveal — a machine gun attached to the plane.*

Wow!

CHAS. We can get this off.

AUDREY. How?

CHAS. Me Collector's Kit.

> CHAS *scrambles down and opens up his satchel.*

Me dad's second-best saw.

> CHAS *holds up the hacksaw.*

Come on, Cem. Audrey, shine this.

> CHAS *throws* AUDREY *a torch. She turns it on and points it at the gun.*

AUDREY. I don't know about this. Should we not get to school?

CEM. Aye, Chas. I don't want any more detentions cos of you.

CHAS. Off you go then if youse not brave enough.

AUDREY. I will.

CHAS. If you go, mind out for all the other dead 'uns in the wood, waiting to get you.

AUDREY. Aw, shurrup.

CEM. Let's get this over with. Quick, Chas!

> AUDREY *watches the boys failing to cut the metal.*

AUDREY. You're not doing it right, you know.

CHAS. You could saw better, could yer?

AUDREY. I could get that off in half the time.

Let us do it.

CHAS. No, this is man's work.

CEM. Keep shining the light, Audrey, I cannet see!

AUDREY. If you're not giving us a go, I'm off then.

CHAS. Ah don't mind.

CEM. Leave us the light at least.

AUDREY. I have to find my way home. Might be other dead Germans, remember.

CEM. Ah lad!

Exit AUDREY, *with the torch.*

CHAS. Girls!

* * *

Lights up on FATTY, *stalking the wood with a dog. The dog barks.*

FATTY. I know you're round here. Come out, kids. Don't make me have to drag youse out.

* * *

CEM. Quick, Chas, Fatty's coming!

CHAS. I'm going as fast as I can!

CEM. Saw faster!

CHAS *saws at the gun turret and the gun comes loose in* CEM'*s hands. It's very heavy.*

Wow!

CHAS. Very nice.

CEM. Heavy.

CHAS. With this I'll have the best collection of war souvenirs in Garmouth.

CEM. You will?

CHAS. Aye. I'm keeping it.

C'mon, Cem. I'll be better than Boddser. Better than anybody. We're mates right?

CEM. Okay. Cos we're mates.

CEM *passes the gun to* CHAS.

CHAS. Me best friend you are, Cemetery Jones.

* * *

FATTY *blows his whistle. The dog barks.*

* * *

CHAS, *shocked, holds the gun, as if to fire. It explodes into life, spraying bullets in all directions.* CHAS *is knocked off his feet.*

CEM. That's done it!

Run!

CHAS. No, wait.

He won't see us. It's too dark for him.

A bark.

CEM. But not too dark for his dog!

He'll smell us. My dog can sniff out a sausage from fifty yards.

Come on, Chas. That's not worth getting caught for.

CHAS *looks at the gun.*

Forget Boddser. We'll find other souvenirs.

CHAS *takes off his blazer and wraps the gun up.*

Come on, Chas, let's go!

CHAS. Not without the gun.

CEM. Chas! We've got to go now. Leg it!

CHAS (*T/A*). And we do. We leg it. Through the dark wood

Keeping ourselves cloaked in shadows of trees and walls

We run through bogs and puddles of mud and gunk

The whole time carrying the gun steady.

The machine gun in my arms.

My machine gun, in my arms.

* * *

3 November. Early morning. The playground of Garmouth High School.

Enter LIDDELL *in his master's gown. He rings his bell and exits.*

Enter CEM *and* CHAS *dressed in school uniform with satchels and gas canisters.*

CHAS (*T/A*). Morning, the next day. And back to school.

Me and Cem in the playground.

CEM. So where is it?

CHAS. I've buried it. I was sure me dad was gonna find it.

CEM. You've got to lose it.

CHAS. I cannet.

CEM. Yer have to. Mam says there's police swarming all over the crash site. It's a matter of time before they find a machine gun's missing.

CHAS. How will they know we've got it?

CEM. Won't take long.

Everyone knows you collect souvenirs.

If I was them I would come straight to you. Or Boddser.

CHAS. They won't if we keep our lips sealed and our mouths shut.

CEM. I don't know, Chas. It's dead risky. Yer know I cannet keep a secret.

CHAS. You've got to. Promise me you'll say nowt?

Enter BODDSER, *wearing round glasses and a military haircut.*

CEM. Oh no!

BODDSER. Morning, McGill. Seen this?

CHAS. Seen what?

BODDSER *shows them a leather flying helmet.*

BODDSER. Nice eh?

CHAS. Doesn't look like much to me.

BODDSER. Don't play stupid, McGill. This is a genuine German flying helmet.

CEM. Where did yer get it?

BODDSER. Wouldn't yer like to know.

CEM. West Chirton Wood, I bet.

BODDSER. How does he know?

CHAS. Heard a plane crashed there.

BODDSER. Yep, with the pilot still inside it. Dead as a dodo.

Look what I got from his pockets.

BODDSER *shows them a fistful of Reichsmarks.*

Reichsmarks! And best of the lot.

BODDSER *shows them a photograph of a young woman.*

Says her name 'Mein Leibling' on the back. Must have been his sweetheart.

She won't be getting any you-know-what for a while.

Not bad, eh?

Bet you'd love something like this, wouldn't yer?

BODDSER *flaps the photo in* CHAS's *face.*

Wouldn't yer?

CEM. Aye, but he's got –

BODDSER. Got what?

CHAS. Nowt.

CEM. Aye, nowt.

BODDSER. Well, McGill, looks like I've still got the best collection of war souvenirs in Garmouth.

And you are still number two.

If you want to be the best, McGill, you've got to be brave. Take a risk.

Something you just haven't got the guts for.

BODDSER *makes chicken-clucking noises as he exits.* CHAS *and* CEM *pull faces and make insulting signs behind* BODDSER*'s back.*

CHAS (*T/A*). That is Boddser.

CHAS *spits on the ground.*

* * *

Classroom at Garmouth High School.

CHAS, CEM, AUDREY *and* CLOGGER *stand to attention behind their desks.*

LIDDELL *reads out the register.*

LIDDELL. Chas McGill?

CHAS. Here, Mr Liddell.

LIDDELL. Cyril Jones?

CEM. Here, Mr Liddell.

LIDDELL. Benjamin Nichol?

Audrey Parton?

AUDREY. Here, Mr Liddell.

LIDDELL. And you, you're new. Who are you?

CLOGGER. Clogger Duncan, sir.

LIDDELL. And your real name?

CLOGGER. Just Clogger.

LIDDELL. And where are you from?

CLOGGER. Glasgae, sir.

My mammy's dead and my daddy's in the Navy.

I'm down here staying with my auntie, sir. For the duration.

LIDDELL. Fall in with these three. And keep an eye on them for me.

LIDDELL *snaps the register shut*.

CLOGGER. What d'ye mean, sir?

LIDDELL (*wearily*). McGill here's got a habit of forgetting to turn up for class. And it seems to be spreading.

A detention is pending for all three of you.

NICKY *comes running in, socks rolled down, shirt untucked*.

At last, Nichol!

NICKY. Sorry, sir!

LIDDELL. Better late than never.

NICKY *tucks himself in*. LIDDELL *unrolls a poster-sized picture of the machine gun*.

Now pay attention.

Who knows what this is?

NICKY. A gun, sir.

LIDDELL. Yes but not any old gun. It's a German aircraft machine gun, the MG15, calibre 7.62mm, firing one thousand rounds a minute, effective range one mile.

Capable of killing twenty people with one squeeze of the trigger.

Constable Hardy was in my office this morning. He tells me one of them's gone missing.

CHAS *kicks* CEM.

CEM. Ow!

LIDDELL. Jones? You know anything about it?

CEM. No, sir.

LIDDELL. McGill?

CHAS *shakes his head.*

Parton?

AUDREY. Erm…

LIDDELL. You do? Do you, Parton? Do you know something?

CHAS *releases the button on his short trousers and they fall to his ankles.*

CHAS. Oh no!

The children laugh.

LIDDELL. For goodness' sake, McGill. Have you not got a belt?

CHAS. It's cardboard, sir. And I think it's gone rotten.

CHAS *grins, mischievously.* LIDDELL *is flustered.*

LIDDELL. Well, pull your trousers up, for God's sake!

CHAS *pulls his trousers up.*

Anyway, the gun. The gun would be quite an addition to any collection, should anyone ever find one.

Time for a bit of public-speaking practice, I think. I'd like a one-minute speech on the subject of…

…war souvenirs.

The children share a look.

CEM. He's for it now.

LIDDELL. Starting with… McGill.

CHAS. Me, sir?

LIDDELL *points to where he wants* CHAS *to stand.* CHAS *steps forward and thinks.*

LIDDELL. Yes please.

CHAS. I used to have the best collection of war souvenirs in Garmouth.

But it is now second best because Boddser Brown in class 3B has beaten me.

He has a 3.7-inch nose-cone, lots of German money with Hitler's face on it and a picture of some pilot's girl called Mein Leibling. Oh, and a pongy German flier's helmet.

I don't know where he got these things.

I'm not really interested in souvenirs any more. I might start collecting cigarette cards.

LIDDELL. McGill, did you say a flying helmet?

CHAS. Did I? Then yes, sir.

LIDDELL. And Brown's got one?

CEM. Yes, sir. Boasting how he found it in West Chirton Wood, sir.

CHAS. The same day that Heinkel crashed, sir.

LIDDELL. Class dismissed.

Nichol, run to reception and tell them I want to speak to Constable Hardy immediately.

Exit NICKY *and* CLOGGER.

* * *

The school playground.

CHAS, AUDREY *and* CEM *enter.*

CHAS. Ha ha, got him. Dropped him right in it!

CEM. He fell for it. Hook. Line. And sinker!

CHAS. Stinker!

They slap hands in celebration.

AUDREY. Think he'll be in trouble?

CHAS. Right now, I'd say.

CEM. Bet Fatty Hardy's squeezing the truth out of him.

CHAS. Squashing the truth out of him.

AUDREY. I wouldn't be too proud of yourselves. When the
police find out Boddser's not got the gun, they'll be right
round yours.

CEM. That's true, Chas.

CHAS. No they won't.

AUDREY. Aye they will.

CEM. Yer better get to yer house before they do.

AUDREY. Immediately!

* * *

The living room in the McGill house.

FATTY *is inspecting* CHAS*'s cardboard box of war
souvenirs and* JACK *watches him, seething.*

FATTY. This everything, is it, Mr McGill?

JACK. –

FATTY. All his souvenirs?

JACK. –

FATTY. When did you say he's back?

JACK *shrugs*

JACK. You want to tell me what all this is about?

FATTY. I'd rather keep that between me and Charles.

Enter CHAS. *He freezes when he sees* FATTY *and* JACK.

JACK. Aye well, speak of the devil.

Chas.

JACK *clicks his fingers and points to his side, beckoning him over.* CHAS *walks over to the adults.* FATTY *opens his notebook and licks the end of his pencil.*

FATTY. Are you Charles Harold McGill?

JACK. No, he's Charlie Peace the Burglar. Cut the cackle, man, and ask proper questions.

FATTY. I'd prefer it if you didn't interfere with my –

I recognise this lad.

JACK *spits into the fireplace.*

JACK. Well, get on with then. I'll be late for my warden's post as it is.

FATTY. If I'm not mistaken, I saw you down West Chirton yesterday. At the laundry.

And you sent me on a wild goose chase.

JACK. Did yer?

CHAS. No.

JACK. Chas?

CHAS. There was a propeller blade there, Dad. I wanted it for me collection and knew Fatty… I mean, Constable Hardy wouldn't let me.

FATTY. He's cunning.

JACK. Like all lads.

FATTY. Not all lads. Some have respect for authority.

CHAS. Hey, that's me collection there. What are you – ?

JACK. Yer better check it, Chas. The thieving git's probably nicked half.

FATTY. This all of your collection, is it, Charles?

CHAS. Aye. Second best in Garmouth.

FATTY. There's nothing else? Something bigger?

CHAS. No.

FATTY. Sure? Then why do you look so guilty?

FATTY *studies* CHAS, *who hangs his head.*

If you've got nothing to say, I'll be off. And this lot will have to come with me.

CHAS. But it's mine. I've been collecting them for months! All the kids in Garmouth have got 'em.

FATTY. The nation needs scrap metal.

JACK. Let the bairn keep them, Constable.

CHAS. Aye, let us keep them!

FATTY. They're the property of the Crown.

CHAS. What does the King want with them?! They're mine!

FATTY *picks up the box of souvenirs.*

FATTY. Think you better get this young man to bed, sir. He's getting quite hysterical.

JACK. Just like a bobby. Pinch all a kid's treasures then blame him for crying.

FATTY. We're looking for a bigger souvenir, Charles. A machine gun. An incredibly dangerous machine gun.

It must be found and returned before somebody gets hurt.

Let us know if anything turns up.

You never know, you might even get these back.

JACK. Get lost!

CHAS. Yeah, get lost.

FATTY *exits*

JACK. You'll get others, lad.

Nowt but a coward, him, picking on kids.

CHAS. Dad, if I was bigger, I tell ya, I would've swung for him. I would've. I would've knocked his head off.

JACK. He's a bobby, Chas. Punch him and you'd be locked in the clink.

CHAS. I don't care! He doesn't understand what they mean. It's not fair.

He's a coward!

* * *

The air-raid siren whines. CHAS *and* MAGGIE *sit in their shelter. Bombs fall and explode. The sound of bricks falling, walls crashing, beams snapping. Screams from terrified women and children. Shouts from wardens, fathers.*

CHAS *(T/A)*. That night there's a raid. Not a normal raid but much worse, the worst so far.

Hour after hour.

Bomb after bomb.

It's like a giant's pounding across the town, his heavy boots crushing everything beneath him.

And we sit, waiting, waiting for his giant boot to stamp down on top of us.

MAGGIE *looks out of the shelter door.*

MAGGIE. That'll be Saville Street gone, they're saying.

Ritz Cinema's gone too.

There won't be any town left by morning.

MAGGIE *looks out of the door again, up to the sky.*

And here's them coming again!

MAGGIE *pulls her head back inside the shelter.*

Where's our guns? Where's the fighters?

We've got no one fighting back!

A bomb drops very near.

CHAS. Are we gonna die, Mam?

MAGGIE. No, course not. We'll be fine.

MAGGIE *fetches the bottle of brandy and begins pouring.*

CHAS. Are we?

They're getting closer and closer.

It's never been as heavy as this before.

Colin Spalding says the Germans are softening us up for the knockout blow.

Ready for invasion.

MAGGIE. Don't listen to a word that lad says. He's full of all sorts of rubbish from that gossip of a mother.

CHAS. He says we'll know they've landed cos Father Coyne will ring the church bells at Holy Saviours.

MAGGIE. Sssh!

A voice (off) shouts 'Bathgate Street's hit.' MAGGIE pours some brandy. Other voices (off) shout 'Chemist's gone', 'Clarke's on fire', 'Nag's Head's down', etc. MAGGIE gives a brandy to CHAS. CHAS drinks it and pulls a face. But he persists because it's adult.

Another explosion.

Oh God.

CHAS. Mam, I'm really [scared].

MAGGIE (*short*). Sssh, Chas. We'll be fine.

Yer dad's on searchlights tonight. He'll be out there lighting up those bombers like Christmas trees.

The RAF will hit them before they even get to us.

Another bomb, this time, huge.

CHAS. Where are the RAF? I cannet hear them.

And why aren't our gunners shooting them down?

MAGGIE. It's hard to hit a plane from the ground.

CHAS. I don't think so. If you light them up properly.

MAGGIE. It's pitch black. I'm sure yer dad's lot are doing their best.

CHAS. I could hit them.

MAGGIE. Don't talk nonsense, Chas. You're a bairn.

CHAS. Easily. When I'm sixteen, I'll sign up. I'll go to Billing's Mill. And take them all down.

MAGGIE. No, I don't think so.

CHAS. Why not? Granddad fought in the last war. At Caparetto.

MAGGIE. And it near killed him. I won't have you fighting.

CHAS. Why not?

MAGGIE. Because… I don't know what me and yer dad would do if you weren't here.

CHAS. But, Mam. Seriously. I want to. I'm not a shacker like Fatty Hardy.

MAGGIE. Well, you don't need worry yourself. This war will be over soon. Very soon.

CHAS. But what if it's not?

The noise of explosions continues then fades.

* * *

Morning. The following day.

CHAS *steps out of the shelter, his hair unkempt. He's tired.*

CHAS (*T/A*). Day breaks across Garmouth

And I step, stiff and shivering out the shelter

It all seems normal

The birds sing morning

Trees, bushes line the garden

Our house is still standing

A quilt of cloud covers the sky

But there – (*Points.*)

Two doors down

There's a gap

A space where two houses used to be.

Fat Ronnie Boyce lived there. With his shiny boots and asthmatic mam.

Gone.

Where's he now?

In Heaven or what?

Enter JACK *in his warden's uniform, looking exhausted.*

It's not fair. Is it?

He's alive, then he's not.

How could God allow that?

I hate Hitler. I hate him.

JACK. Chassy, chum us over to your nana and granda's.

CHAS. They're not dead an' all?

JACK. No, they had a lucky escape. The roof's caved in and they need helping back to ours. They'll live in our front room.

CHAS. But what if a bomb hits ours? We'll all be dead.

JACK *rubs his face, tired.*

JACK. Hmm? That's fate. There's nowt we can do about that.

CHAS. No, there is. Isn't there?

Dad?

JACK *shrugs.*

(*T/A.*) We can. It's time to do something about it.

To fight back.

I start hatching a plan.

* * *

Playground. Garmouth High School. Afternoon.

CHAS *has his satchel and gas-mask case. He is joined by*
CEM *and* CLOGGER.

CEM. So why are we doing this?

CLOGGER. Aye, what's this about, McGill?

CHAS. You'll see. I've got a plan brewing.

CEM. To do with the gun, I bet.

CHAS. Just follow everything I do and we'll be fine.

CEM. I'm sure! Every time I follow one of your ideas, I get in
    trouble.

CHAS (*T/A*). First stop. Sicky Nicky. Really skinny and always
    snotty. His dad was a sea captain so his family's rich. In this
    school, though, being posh is definitely not a good thing.

Lights on NICKY, *who is preparing himself for the fight
ahead.*

Good afternoon, Nichol, my dear chap.

NICKY. What do you want?

CHAS. A quiet word in yer lug – if you have a moment.

NICKY. There's no point you picking on me too, McGill. Boddser's about to have his go.

CHAS. It's about Boddser we wanted to speak to yer.

NICKY. I don't care. Whatever you say won't make any difference.

CHAS. We're gonna stop him.

CEM. Are we?

NICKY. How?

CLOGGER. Yeah, how?

CHAS. As you leave this schoolyard, what's Boddser going to do?

NICKY. Trip me up at the school gates and steal my money.

CHAS. He's not. Cos we are going to protect yer. Like a convoy. Across the playground, through the gates and all the way home.

CEM (to CHAS). You're mad. Boddser's a foot taller than either of us. How we gonna get past him?

CHAS. Clogger.

CLOGGER. Me?

CHAS. Aye. He plays scrum half and once played a whole match after losing two front teeth.

CLOGGER. I'm no' into fighting, Chas. I've seen enough violence in my life, man.

CHAS. C'mon, Clogger!

CLOGGER. No chance. You're on your own, wee man.

CHAS. But you've got to! He'd never fight you. But he'd kill me!

CLOGGER. Tough.

CEM. Chas –

Enter BODDSER. *He blocks the gang's path.* CHAS *steps in front of* NICKY.

BODDSER. Look what we have here. Chas McGill and his new girlfriend.

How sweet you look.

CHAS. Get lost, Boddser.

BODDSER. No. You get lost. He's mine. To do whatever I like with.

CHAS. I beg your pardon, Four-eyes. I should bow down to your magnificence!

BODDSER. Getaway, McGill. I'm warning yer. I've no quarrel with you, for now. Hand him over.

CHAS. Oh I am so scared. I think I've wet me pants.

BODDSER. Right, then you're asking for it.

BODDSER *puts his bag down and raises his fists.*

CEM. Bloody fool, Chas.

CHAS *looks over his shoulder to* CLOGGER, *who shakes his head. He's on his own.*

CHAS. You better take your specs off first. I divnt want yer ape of a mother complaining to me dad if I break them!

BODDSER *takes his glasses off and raises his fists.*

(*T/A*). And so I swing a first punch

My fingers bunched

In a blind punch

I get him, hit him square in the guts

He doubles, bends, throws his fist

I twist, he misses

I lunge, crunch me nose

Against his elbow

Wrestle

Back, forward, to, fro

Back, forward, to, fro

Push in to

Whirl of arms and fists

And shouts and knees and kicks

Boddser pushes me shoulder

Am pushed forward and over

Down and over

Turned over

Boddser turns me over

Climbs over and sits

On me back, face in the dirt

Fists and arms hit me arms and face

Red mist takes over

Rage takes over

I turn over, push him over

It's real rage. I –

CHAS *springs up, throwing a handful of fine gravel into*
BODDSER*'s eyes.* BODDSER *doubles up.* CHAS *grabs his*
gas-mask case and swings it at BODDSER*'s head. It strikes*
and BODDSER *falls to the ground.* CHAS*, full of murder,*
jumps on BODDSER *and hits him repeatedly around the*
head. CLOGGER *and* CEM *drag* CHAS *off* BODDSER.
CHAS *tries to fight them off.* CLOGGER *grabs* CHAS.
CEM *grabs the gas-mask case.*

CEM. You're mad, Chas. Stop it! Stop it!

CHAS *rests*. CLOGGER *inspects* BODDSER.

CLOGGER. Enough of yer greetin', man. Ye'll live. Ye sound like a wee bairn.

Get yourself to hospital before you bleed out.

(*To* CHAS.) You're stronger than ye ken, Chas.

BODDSER. I'll get you back for this, McGill. I know you've got that gun. I know it. I'll see you're done for it.

BODDSER *slopes off*.

AUDREY. Chas, that wasn't right. Not right at all.

Nazis fight dirty, not us.

Britishers fight with their fists.

CEM. You've become worse than him.

Exit AUDREY, CLOGGER *and* CEM.

* * *

CHAS *is alone on stage. The voices of other characters ring inside his head.*

MAGGIE. I don't know what got in to him, Jack. It's not from us, I'm sure. I'm so ashamed.

JACK. Fighting like a coward that was, lad.

It's yer fists you should use.

LIDDELL. Yes, McGill, British boys fight with their fists. I am very disappointed in you. Very disappointed in you indeed.

CHAS. But I'm small! What are you supposed to do if you're small?

JACK. A coward.

MAGGIE. Coward.

The word 'coward' rings around the stage. LIDDELL *enters with a cane in his hand.*

LIDDELL. Cowardly, McGill. It's six of the best.

> CHAS *holds his hand out in front of him, palm upwards.*
> LIDDELL *strikes the cane down.* CHAS *winces. Sound*
> *effect of a cane striking six times.*

* * *

> *The playground. Garmouth High School.*

> CHAS *sits alone.*

> *Enter* NICKY. *He sits next to* CHAS. *He offers* CHAS *a*
> *sweet from a paper bag.*

NICKY. They're rhubarb and custards.

> CHAS *takes one.*

> What you did before –

CHAS. I know… like a coward. Say what everyone else is
saying.

NICKY. No. It was brave.

> Boddser hasn't picked on us since.

> NICKY *holds his hand out.* CHAS *shakes it.*

> I've got cola drops in my bag and custard creams at my
> house.

> I've got a goldfish too. He's this – (*Indicates fifteen*
> *centimetres.*) long.

CHAS. Yer have not.

NICKY. I have.

CHAS. They always die when they get too big for the jam jar.

NICKY. He's got a pond, all to himself. He's the same age as
me.

CHAS. Aye, whatever yer say.

NICKY. And do you like butter?

CHAS. Aye! I haven't had any since the war started.

NICKY. We've got a mountain of it at my house. My mother gets it off the destroyers.

You wanna come round? You can have as much as you like.

CHAS. Hellish! I'll come round tomorrow.

Exit NICKY.

(*T/A.*) What's not so hellish is life back home. Dad doesn't speak to us for two days. And Mam's got a face on if I even breathe in her direction.

Audrey's the first to forgive us.

I only hope Cem and Clogger don't stay mad for too long.

* * *

The Nichol house. Garden. Afternoon.

Inside the house, a popular wartime song plays on a gramophone. The music drifts out of the open window in to the garden.

AUDREY *looks up at the house.* CHAS *pokes a stick into the green fish pond.*

AUDREY. It's not like how I thought it would be.

CHAS. How do you mean?

AUDREY. Well –

I mean –

My mam and dad were always going on about 'The Nichol's Place'. They came to one of the garden parties. Mam was going on for weeks about it, saying it was dead grand.

The Mayor was here and me dad's boss. They had cocktails.

Captain Nichol showed me dad his medals. And the statues he'd got from Africa.

They said Nicky's mam was like a film star and Mam felt all funny talking to her.

CHAS. I've seen her.

AUDREY. When?

CHAS. Before. When I went to the lav. She was stood in the dining room, in a dressing gown.

AUDREY. But it's three o'clock.

CHAS. I know. She was just staring out the window.

Beat.

AUDREY. I don't like it here at all. It's like a haunted house. You said he had a fish to look at. But I cannet see owt in here. It's all green.

Let's go. He won't fit in with us lot anyway.

CHAS. No, I'm staying. I like him.

Enter NICKY, *from the house, with a tray holding a jug of lemonade and glasses.*

AUDREY. No, yer don't. You're up to something.

CHAS. Am not.

AUDREY. Chas, you're always up to something. There's something Nicky's got that you want. I'd bet me life on it.

CHAS. Sssh.

NICKY *lays the tray down.*

AUDREY. Was that your mam singing?

NICKY. Yes. Sorry.

AUDREY. She sounded like Vera Lynn.

NICKY. It means she's happy.

NICKY *pours the lemonade into glasses.*

AUDREY. What does yer mam do?

NICKY. Not much since my father was killed.

Sometimes she sits out here and tells me stories about how they met.

As long as I don't get in her way, she lets me do whatever I like.

No one comes here any more.

Apart from sailors.

CHAS. Who was that man in the kitchen?

NICKY. The chap in charge of the ratings. He lives here all the time now.

The children share a look.

AUDREY. So… you've got a goldfish?

NICKY *looks into the murky water.*

NICKY. Somewhere in there. There used to be twelve of them. My father imported them from China but this is the only one left. He's called Oscar.

Here.

NICKY *hands a bag of bread to the gang and they feed the fish.*

CHAS. There he is! '*Ni hao*, Oscar.'

AUDREY. Hello, Oscar. You're very pretty.

CHAS. You have to speak in Chinese to him. He doesn't understand English.

NICKY. Sometimes he does.

I think he's quite clever.

AUDREY *steps to one side.*

Don't stand there, Audrey.

AUDREY. Oh?

NICKY. That's Toby, my cocker spaniel. He's buried there.

And that stone's Mirabel, my first cat.

AUDREY *inspects a cross.*

AUDREY. Who's Monty?

NICKY. My last hamster. He could eat a whole bag of sunflower seeds in one go.

AUDREY. What about that one? There's no name on that.

NICKY. That's for my father.

AUDREY....

CHAS....

> NICKY *sprinkles breadcrumbs on the grave*.

NICKY. I do this every day.

> See, he went down with his ship. It's what captains have to do.

CHAS. That's real bravery, that.

NICKY. Yeah.

> CHAS *steps away and points off*.

CHAS. What's behind those trees at the end of the garden?

AUDREY. The sea, stupid.

NICKY. And the heath. From there you can see the harbour.

CHAS. And that's exactly the way any Germans would come.

AUDREY. No way!

CHAS. Definitely. If they invade they'll come from Norway. And Norway's straight over there.

> CHAS *turns to the gang*.

> Listen. We're mates right?

AUDREY (*suspicious*). Aye.

CHAS. I've got an idea.

AUDREY. Here we go! I knew it. This is always where trouble starts.

CHAS. This place is perfect. Quiet, away from anyone else. Overlooking the sea. Let's make a secret camp at the end of garden.

NICKY. Here?

CHAS. Aye. We'll make it our base and bring chairs and beds and cakes and biscuits.

And have a stove and bunks.

It'll be a fortress, our fortress, and we'll sit out watching for Germans.

NICKY. I've got my father's telescope.

CHAS. So we'll keep watch for German boats.

If they come, we'll call the alarm.

AUDREY. And save Garmouth?

CHAS. Aye, save Garmouth.

What do yer think? Nicky, it's your garden.

NICKY. I like it.

They raise their glasses of lemonade and clink glasses.

CHAS. Nicky, once the fortress is built, there's something else we'd like to bring here.

NICKY. What is it?

CHAS. If we let yer in on a secret, do you promise not to tell anyone?

NICKY *nods his head enthusiastically.*

* * *

Bottom of the Nichols' Garden.

The gang – CHAS, AUDREY and NICKY – begin building Fortress Caparetto.

As they build, they sing 'Pack Up Your Troubles' or a similar rousing song. CEM *and* CLOGGER *enter, and begin helping* AUDREY *and* NICKY. *When* CHAS *sees them, there's an awkward reconciliation – a nod of the head, their help in carrying materials. The whole gang continues singing the song.*

As they build, we hear voices from the community reporting the theft of the materials we see being used.

FATTY. Sir, strange as this sounds – someone's pinching sandbags.

Even the ones dogs pee on, sir!

Must be the work of enemy agents! Bloody Nazi Quislings are stealing our British sand!

MAGGIE. Jack, me best bedsheet –

It's gone missing. I could swear I washed it…

JACK. Maggie? Maggie! I divnt believe it, some thieving git's nicked half me cement and a load of bricks!

PETTY OFFICER. I say, Captain, forget about the butter going AWOL. My chaps have lost two fire buckets, one noticeboard, one stove, paraffin, a heater and a pump and stirrup and three tin hats.

* * *

The Fortress. Christmas Eve 1940.

CHAS *is up a tree, scanning the horizon with Captain Nichol's brass telescope.*

He is in the crow's nest wearing a bright-red steel helmet marked 'Caparetto'. It is freezing cold and the wind makes his eyes water. The hard strap of the helmet cuts into his chin.

CLOGGER *listens to a radio,* AUDREY *makes toast on the stove,* CEM *pours mugs of tea,* NICKY *shuffles cards.*

CHAS (*T/A*). School broke up for Christmas so first thing every morning we rushed here and spent the day building.

Two weeks it took us but finally, finally, Fortress Caparetto was ready. Named after the place me granddad fought in the Great War and complete with roof, bunks, kitchen and table.

Two-foot thick walls and with a clear view over the North Sea.

I was Captain and kept watch for Germans.

CHAS *jumps down from the crow's nest.*

Petty Officer Duncan took care of intelligence.

CEM *gives* CHAS *toast and tea.*

Private Nichol organised entertainment.

Sergeant Jones made gallons of hot tea.

And Quartermaster Parton made toast on the stove.

AUDREY. Spread with real butter.

CEM. Covers the soot, sir.

CHAS *takes a bite.*

CHAS. That's smashing, that.

(*T/A.*) As the New Year broke, if things couldn't get any better, they did!

CLOGGER. Hey, you lot, listen to this!

CHAS, CEM, NICKY *and* AUDREY *rush over to* CLOGGER *and listen to the wireless.*

You're no' gonna believe it!

AUDREY. What is it?

CHAS. What's happened?

CLOGGER. Sssh!

CEM. I cannet hear. Turn it up!

CHAS. What's it saying?

CLOGGER. Sssh! Sssh!

CLOGGER *turns the dial up*.

RADIO. …and police have confirmed that yesterday evening a German plane crashed into the roof of Garmouth High School. We understand that the school will be closed for the foreseeable future. There is no word yet what provision will be made for the school's eight hundred pupils.

The gang cheer. CLOGGER *turns the radio off*.

CEM. All my prayers have been answered. There is a God!

CLOGGER. You know what this means?

AUDREY. We can stay here for as long we like!

NICKY. Yeah!

CLOGGER. Aye, we can dae what we like with nobody telling us what to dae apart from us!

CEM. Thank you, Luftwaffe. I'm so happy I could even kiss Audrey.

AUDREY. Yuck! No thank you.

CEM. I've got a sloppy one here for you, pet lamb!

CEM *makes to kiss* AUDREY. *She runs away from him.*

It's got yer name on it!

AUDREY. Gerraway, yer silly fool.

CEM. All right, I'll just have to kiss Clogger!

CLOGGER. No chance, Jones! Unless ye want a Glasgae kiss back?

They grin.

NICKY. Hey, why don't we have a party?

CHAS. Aye!

NICKY. Around a campfire. Here.

AUDREY. We can have sausages.

CHAS. And roast marshmallows!

CLOGGER. Covered in chocolate.

CEM. Aye, sausages covered in marshmallow and chocolate.

AUDREY. Eurrgh! You are disgusting.

> CEM *laughs and begins a silly dance with* NICKY. CHAS *steps into the crow's nest.*

CEM. Tell yer what, yer better get yer best dancing dress on, Audrey. This afternoon is party time at Fortress Caparetto.

CLOGGER. Aye, let's get some wood for the campfire, eh.

> CEM *stops dancing.*

AUDREY. Come on, yer silly fool!

> You can help us get sausages from the house.

> *Exit* CLOGGER *and* AUDREY.

CEM. Are you coming, Chas?

CHAS. No, Sergeant. I'm gonna watch out for the enemy.

> There's been sneak raiders near teatime every day this week.

CEM. What about you, Nicky?

NICKY. I'll go and get some plates.

CEM. And the marshmallows, don't forget!

NICKY. I won't!

> CEM *salutes* NICKY, *who salutes back. He exits.*

> You want anything from the kitchens, Captain?

CHAS. I'm grand here, thank you.

> NICKY *moves to exit but* CHAS *stops him.*

> Wait… Nicky? Will yer mam be all right with us being here. Like, all the time.

> Do you think she'll, you know, want to know what we're doing?

NICKY. No, she's said nothing. She doesn't even know you're here.

> She hasn't been out her room since Tuesday.

CHAS. So you all right with not letting on?

> Yer can say if yer not.

NICKY. Chas, this is better than all right.

> It's… I dunno, it's the best ever.

* * *

CHAS (*T/A*). Good times like that don't last. Especially when there's a war on.

> The bombers come every night.

> And that night something happens

> Something that blows our whole world upside down.

> *The sound of an enormous explosion with timber cracking, tiles smashing and walls crashing down.*

* * *

The Nichols' garden. Morning.

CHAS *stands looking up at the Nichols' house, stunned.*

AUDREY *enters. She too, stares up open-mouthed at the back of the house.* CEM *and* CLOGGER *enter a moment later.*

CEM. Is it true?

CLOGGER. Tell us folk are having a laugh, man, eh.

AUDREY (*shakes her head*). I've been round the whole area. The bomb fell on the roof. It's all caved in. And the whole back of the house is gone.

Totally gone.

CEM. Nicky's bedroom?

Beat.

AUDREY. Gone.

CHAS. So Nicky – ?

AUDREY *shakes her head. The gang look at each other, shocked. Eventually,* CEM *stands and goes to the pond.*

CEM. The pond's hit too. Look at it, all cracked and empty.

CHAS *picks up Oscar the fish.*

AUDREY. Oscar!

CHAS. Dead.

I'm gonna bury him.

CHAS *scrapes at the frozen ground with his fingers.*

AUDREY. Chas?

CHAS. He's got to have a proper funeral.

With dignity.

He shouldn't be just thrown to one side. It's not right.

CHAS *keeps scraping but is getting nowhere. His digging gets more desperate, more upset.*

Damn! It's frozen solid.

CHAS *punches the ground.*

It's not fair, not fair!

CEM. I know, Chas. Nicky was one of us.

AUDREY *puts her hand on* CHAS*'s shoulder.*

CHAS. Nothing in this war is fair. It's like God's turned his head and given up.

Enter NICKY, *from the trees.*

CLOGGER. Hey! Look!

CEM. Look!

CHAS. Nicky! Is that you, man?

AUDREY. We thought you were dead!

NICKY. Everyone else is. My mother, the chap from the ratings.

I found them.

CEM. Where were you?

NICKY. In there.

CHAS. The Fortress?

CLOGGER. In the middle of the night?

CHAS. How come?

NICKY. Don't laugh. But last night my father appeared in my dream. He warned me to get out the house.

AUDREY *puts her hand on* NICKY, *a bit awkwardly.*

It's like he knew that something bad was going to happen.

And it did.

CLOGGER. Ah, Nicky, man.

NICKY. I'm okay.

CHAS. Here ya.

CHAS *pulls a bag of mints out of his pocket and* NICKY *takes one, then two.*

Have two if you like.

AUDREY. What're you gonna do now?

NICKY. I don't know. There's no one else in our family. I suppose they'll put me in a home.

CHAS *and* AUDREY *look at each other.* NICKY *walks towards the Fortress.*

I don't want to leave though. You know, the Fortress – it feels more like a home than that house ever did.

AUDREY. We've got to tell some grown-ups.

CLOGGER. No way.

AUDREY. Everyone thinks he's dead. They'll all be worrying.

CLOGGER. Who? Who in this town cares about Nicky, eh?

CEM. I do.

CHAS. Yeah, we all do.

CLOGGER. Not the grown-ups.

AUDREY. But they know best.

CLOGGER. If you think that then you're madder than Uncle Adolf.

They'll do what's best for them. And that'll be tidying him away in a home and forgetting him like they did with me when my ma died. In a home, they give ye porridge without sugar and belt ye if ye leave your shoes lying about.

AUDREY. He could stay with one of us.

CEM. Aye.

CLOGGER. Your ma would have him? Or yours? Or yours?

I know what they thought of his mammy, I've heard ye.

CHAS. You could stay with me but my nana and granddad are living with us. They've got nowhere else to go either.

CEM. He's got to live somewhere.

NICKY. I want to live here.

AUDREY. In the Fortress?

NICKY. There's lots of food in the old stables. That petty officer was in the black market. There's loads of tins and packets, everything.

CHAS. It's not going to last long.

NICKY. Enough for a year I reckon.

CLOGGER. I've known folks put up with worse in Glasgow.

CEM. What if he gets ill?

CLOGGER. Then we'll take him to the doctor's.

AUDREY. But won't he get lonely?

NICKY hangs his head and cries. AUDREY puts her hand on him.

All do this.

The gang put their hands on NICKY. CLOGGER sits and puts his arm around NICKY.

CLOGGER. You'll no' get lonely. Cos I'll be here, living with ye.

CHAS. In there?

CLOGGER. Why not?

CEM. Your auntie.

AUDREY. She'll miss you.

CLOGGER. To hell with her. She's no' even my real auntie. Just my mother's cousin. And she never wanted me in the first place. I've had enough of sleeping three in a bed, with no clean clothes and no' enough to eat. The only thing she'll miss is the money my da sends.

AUDREY. Does she not love you?

CLOGGER. Love me? What's love? All she and ma 'uncle' love is their beer and fags. I've been wanting to run away for weeks.

AUDREY. I still –

CLOGGER. Where were they when the bomb dropped on Nicky's house?

They couldn't save the house.

Just like they couldn't save Poland, Norway or France.

We saved him. In our Fortress. Built by us.

It's all now up to us.

As far as I'm concerned, this is home.

The others nod.

And we look after each other.

No parents. Just us.

CHAS. Fortress Caparetto.

CEM. Aye, Fortress Caparetto!

CHAS fetches the gun and places it on the ground. The gang gather round it.

CHAS. Everyone. Swear on the gun.

This is our fortress.

A fortress to defend our nation.

And everyone who lives in it.

ALL. Fortress Caparetto! Fortress Caparetto! Fortress –

CEM. Everyone sssh!

AUDREY. Cyril!

CEM. No, listen.

They all quieten and listen.

CHAS. What?

NICKY. I can't hear anything.

CEM. That.

CHAS. Cem, what?

CEM. Can you not hear it? Engines.

CLOGGER. Give me the telescope.

CLOGGER *moves to look out to sea with the telescope.*

I'll be damned. A Jerry plane, north by north-east, and it's flying low. Four miles out I'd say.

CEM. Coming towards us?

CLOGGER. Directly.

AUDREY. Tell the Home Guard.

CHAS. No.

AUDREY. Chas, what should we / do?

CHAS. Too late.

It's up to us.

Set the gun!

CEM. Set the gun!

AUDREY, NICKY *and* CEM *grab the gun.* CLOGGER *retreats behind* CHAS.

The gang set the gun up, resting its muzzle on a sandbag. They point the gun out to sea.

CLOGGER. Two miles, approaching.

NICKY. I can't see it.

CLOGGER. You will. Wait. It's a twin-engined bomber.

AUDREY. Where is it?

CEM *points out to sea.*

CHAS. There.

CLOGGER. One mile, approaching.

CHAS. It's a British plane. A Blenheim.

CLOGGER. No, it's a Messerschmitt. Definitely a Nazi.

CEM *points off inland.*

CEM. What's that? Two o'clock!

CLOGGER *looks through the telescope.*

AUDREY. Is it a Spitfire?

CLOGGER. Aye, a Spitfire, but it's never gonna make it in time.

CHAS. Prepare the gun.

CEM *releases the safety catch.*

CEM. Preparing the gun.

CHAS. Secured?

CEM. Secured.

CHAS. Ammunition loaded?

CEM. Ammunition loaded.

AUDREY. He's coming!

CHAS. Taking aim.

CEM. Safe positions, company.

NICKY. Kill him!

CLOGGER. Five hundred yards approaching.

CLOGGER *retreats behind the gun.* AUDREY *puts her fingers in her ears. The plane thunders towards them.*

NICKY. Fire, Chas! Kill him.

CEM. Prepare to fire.

CHAS. Ready to fire.

NICKY. Fire, Chas!

CLOGGER. Now, Chas, now!

> CHAS *fires the gun. The gang watch the plane as it loops one way, then the next, before going into a tailspin.*

NICKY. Got him! You got him, Chas!

CEM. It's spinning.

AUDREY. It's falling.

NICKY. It's falling.

CLOGGER. It's –

> *The plane crashes, with an orange glow. The gang bounce up and down and cheer.*

* * *

> *A searchlight catches a pilot with a parachute descending to earth.*

ACT TWO

A wood. Morning.

RUDI – *a German pilot – is hanging upside down, tangled in his parachute. He struggles, dismantles himself and falls to the ground in a heap. He stands, removes his goggles, and dusts himself down. He looks around furtively.*

He is dressed in a pilot's uniform and sticks out like a sore thumb. He quickly bundles up the parachute and limps off.

* * *

The Fortress.

CEM *makes tea on the stove.* AUDREY *inspects a section of cloth – previously a section of roof.* CHAS *is dismantling and then cleaning the gun with a rag.* CLOGGER *sits in the crow's nest, looking out to sea through the telescope.*

CHAS (*T/A*). Outside the Fortress, I'm buzzing off the thrill of the trigger. Me heart beating, hands sweating, legs like strawberry jelly.

But, it's safe to say the others aren't exactly celebrating our first hit.

AUDREY. I hope you're pleased with yourself. You've blown a great big hole in our roof with that gun.

CEM. But we got him!

AUDREY. No yer never. Youse two missed him by miles.

CEM. We brought him down. You saw him crash over there.

AUDREY. Yeah, but it was that Spitfire that hit him. Ye knar, the one that was flying behind him, firing on target.

CEM. But –

CHAS. Aye, that was just a practice go. We'll get him next time.

AUDREY. Next time you'll kill someone.

CHAS. That's what we're trying to do!

AUDREY. I'm not talking about Nazis, I'm talking about one of us! Them bullets went everywhere.

CHAS. Aye, cos that laughing fool jogged me arm.

CEM. Me? I was holding it steady. The problem is you're too puny to control it.

CHAS. Nobody could've held it. It kicks like a mule. As you'd know if you had the guts to fire it.

CEM. I have got guts.

CHAS. Have not.

CEM. Have so.

CHAS. Have not.

CEM. Have so.

CHAS. Have not.

CEM. Have so.

CLOGGER. Ach, you three! Shut it, for God's sake. You're nippin' ma heed.

CLOGGER *gets down from the crow's nest. He takes a mug of tea.*

Chas… I mean, Captain… that gun's got to be secured before it's fired again. The quartermaster's right. One of us could have been shot.

We can't afford to lose men and women at this stage.

CHAS. I know.

We'll get a tripod or something to hold this.

CLOGGER. Good.

Now let's keep it down, eh. Nichol's asleep.

AUDREY. He must be knackered.

CHAS. Aye.

AUDREY. I'll have some of that hot water for cocoa. He'll like that.

CLOGGER. Keep him warm and watch for bad dreams. That home I was in, kids suffered awful from nightmares.

CEM. Here.

CEM *passes a mug of tea to* CHAS. *And then another cup to* AUDREY.

I've got to get home soon. Me dad's getting suspicious.

AUDREY. Mine too.

CHAS. How come?

CEM. He wants to know why I keep coming home so muddy, when I'm supposed to be at the library. And why I never go in for my dinner.

CHAS. What do you say?

CEM. That I keep falling over. So now he thinks something's wrong with me. He definitely doesn't believe us.

I don't know how long I can keep all this secret.

AUDREY. Nor me. See Fatty Hardy was round ours last night.

CHAS. What did that nosy idiot want?

AUDREY. He was asking loads of questions about you. Where yer go all day, what you do, if you're acting suspiciously.

CHAS. What did you say?

AUDREY. That I'm a proper lady and I hate hanging out with smelly boys.

CLOGGER. Good. Cos we've got to be clever. Tell nobody nothing – and I mean nothing – about this place. As far as any adult is concerned, Nicky's dead, I've done a runner and your days are spent in the library or fishing.

CHAS. And keep changing your journeys from your house to here.

CLOGGER. Zigzags.

CHAS. Go down alleyways and through hedges. This place has got to stay secret.

CLOGGER. So we can stay here for good.

AUDREY. Are you really not going home?

CLOGGER. Never. This is home for me now.

CHAS. You're not going to say anything are yer, Cem?

CEM. I divnt know how long I can hold him off.

CHAS. You'll have to try, Cem. And you, Audrey.

AUDREY. I can't lie to me dad, Chas. And nor can you, I know.

CLOGGER. Dinnae worry what yer daddies think. Remember we're your family now.

Stay united and we'll be as safe as houses here.

* * *

The warden's post.

LIDDELL *strides into the room at pace, a report under his arm, followed by* FATTY.

LIDDELL. Constable, I've told you I can't be any help.

FATTY. But, Mr Liddell –

LIDDELL. Really, like I said, the school is closed. And until it reopens, my duties are here.

Not as a schoolteacher but as a warden, in charge of this post.

FATTY. Sir, you're not –

LIDDELL. Listening?

Look, Constable, you don't need me to tell you there's a war on. And there are more important things for me to do than help you search for a missing gun.

FATTY. But your pupils have it.

LIDDELL. So where is it then? I helped you identify Brown and McGill. If you couldn't get it from them then –

FATTY. Yes, but –

LIDDELL. But what, Constable?

FATTY. They know you. You can get intelligence out of them that I can't. I need you to find out where they're hiding it.

LIDDELL. But you don't even know they've got it.

FATTY. Oh I do. I know McGill's got the gun. It's written all over his face. And his little friends are in on it too.

FATTY *flips open his notebook.*

The parents of Parton and Jones say their kids are out the house for hours on end. And come back each night tired and dirty.

The Duncan boy has been missing for a week now with no sight of him here or Glasgow.

LIDDELL. You're not suggesting they're hiding the Duncan boy?

FATTY. Yes. Those kids are together and they've got that gun.

I know it.

LIDDELL. Look, even if you're right, this gun is just a souvenir for these kids. For showing off. There's no way they'd be stupid enough to fire it.

FATTY. Is that right?

FATTY *opens his hand to display some flattened bullets.*

Bullets, sir.

German bullets. Fired the same day that bomber crashed near the harbour.

LIDDELL. And?

FATTY. Found embedded in the wall of an old lady's bedroom.

LIDDELL. Probably from a German plane?

FATTY. She lives on the ground floor, sir. Unless the Messerschmitt was parked outside her house, these were fired from a machine gun on ground level.

One inch lower and she'd be dead.

FATTY *gives the bullets to* LIDDELL.

It's a killing machine, Mr Liddell.

This gang must be caught and arrested.

Help me find them.

LIDDELL *passes* FATTY *his binoculars*.

LIDDELL. Here, take these.

Follow those kids and watch where they go.

If… if you're right, then come back to me. We'll mobilise the Home Guard.

But for God's sake, Constable, get over this obsession. You have a duty, remember.

FATTY. This is my duty, sir. I won't stop till that gang is found and arrested.

* * *

The Fortress.

The gang are sitting around the machine gun, which is now supported on a tripod.

AUDREY *cuts up plain biscuits and then hands them out.*
NICKY *sits on the bunk, shuffling cards.*

CHAS. Go on then, test it. Took me dad ages to make it. I told him it was to hold a telescope.

CLOGGER *waggles the gun. It doesn't move.*

CLOGGER. Aye, it's better, much better.

Snug as a bug in a rug.

CHAS. Nice and safe.

CLOGGER. Might as well change the magazines, eh.

CEM. I'll do that.

CHAS. No, I will.

CHAS *carefully, nervously, takes the gun off the tripod and…*

CLOGGER. Easy now. These things go off.

CHAS. Okay.

…removes the empty magazine.

CEM. Yer want me to test it while it's empty?

CHAS *picks up the gun, much to* CEM*'s annoyance, and pulls the lever.*

CHAS. There. Working nicely.

CEM. Give us a go then, Chas.

CHAS. It works.

CEM. I know but I wanna go. Be like John Wayne as the Ringo Kid!

CLOGGER. Ach!

CEM. Go on, Chas. Mates, eh?

CHAS. If you must.

CEM. Yeah!

CEM *lifts the gun and poses with it.*

What do you think? Do I look like John Wayne?

NICKY. More like Desperate Dan.

AUDREY. Very desperate.

CLOGGER. Put it down, Cem.

CEM. Why? What's the worst that can happen?

CHAS. Just put it down, eh.

AUDREY. Nicky's starting a game of Gin Rummy.

CEM *points the gun at* AUDREY.

CEM. It's got no bullets in it. There's no need to wet your knickers.

AUDREY. Cem! You've got to put it down!

Put it down!

CEM *is taken aback by the strength of* AUDREY*'s voice. Awkward moment.*

You're not a kid any more.

CEM *– trying to salvage some pride – points the gun out and pulls the lever. It jams.* CEM *tries to pull the lever again. Jammed.*

CHAS. You've jammed it! It's broken!

CEM. No, I haven't! It's just… it's not working this time but… if yer pull this then / it'll just –

CEM *pulls the lever harder. A shower of tiny pieces fall over the floor.*

CLOGGER. Ach, you've bust it proper now!

AUDREY. Cem!

CEM. I didn't. It was… it was broken before I touched it. It was you that did it.

CHAS. Was not.

CEM. Was so. All I was doing was / the same as what you did –

AUDREY. Well done, Cyril / very clever.

AUDREY *begins searching and collecting the pieces.*
CLOGGER *joins her.*

CLOGGER. What use is a gun that can't fire?

CEM. Wasn't my fault.

CLOGGER. Was so, man.

CHAS. You're always such a child.

CEM. And you're not?

CHAS. No!

CEM. You're the one who brought those *Dandy* comics. And always wants to play stupid card games.

CHAS. Am I? Who's the one who still plays with a train set and who mashes up all his food like a little baby? Not me, I'm telling you.

AUDREY. Captain! We've got to be better than this. We cannet act like six-year-olds always arguing about stupid things.

Help me pick up the pieces and stop bickering.

CHAS. I'm not bickering. He's the one bickering.

CEM. I'm not –

CLOGGER. We're missing the spring. It cannae have gone far. Help us look.

CHAS (*to* NICKY). Are you gonna help or what?

NICKY. Yeah, sure...

CHAS *and* NICKY *get down on their knees searching for bits of the gun.* CEM *holds the light over them.*

AUDREY. I saw a nut go this way.

CLOGGER. Forget that, for God's sake. It's the spring we want. What about under here?

AUDREY. I dunno. I can't tell cos it's such a tip in here. It looks like a pigsty. There's rubbish everywhere. Your clothes and dirty plates.

CLOGGER. Ach, I cannae find it.

CLOGGER *gives up*.

CEM. Oh lad, this is a disaster. What's the point in looking?

I mean, we've got a damp shelter with no gun and the only nice food left are some old biscuits! I've had enough with this, I reckon we should pack up and go home.

CHAS (*simultaneous*). Cem?!

AUDREY (*simultaneous*). Cem?!

ALL. Shut up!

NICKY, *facing away from the entrance, picks up the spring. At the same time, enter* RUDI, *who stumbles in and stops*.

NICKY. Found it!

NICKY *turns round.* AUDREY *gasps and points*.

I found the spring!

CHAS *grabs the machine gun and points it at* RUDI. RUDI *puts his hands up*.

CEM. It's a Jerry. Get his gun!

RUDI (*shakes his head*). *Dummkopf!*

CLOGGER *springs into action, getting behind* RUDI, *patting him around the waist.* CLOGGER *flips open the holster and pulls out a Luger pistol. He trains the gun on* RUDI.

CLOGGER. *Hände hoch!*

You're under arrest, mate. Don't try any funny business or we'll, you know, have to… we will.

AUDREY. Who are yer? And what are yer doing / in England?

CEM. A Nazi pig.

Shoot him before he kills us.

You've heard what Nazis are like. They kill kids and do bad things to nuns.

CHAS *shakes his head*.

RUDI. *Bitte… Ich muss…* sit… tired. Very tired.

The gang looks to each other.

CEM. On yer knees though.

RUDI *nods and kneels, his hands behind his head*.

CHAS. Keep a watch on him, Petty Officer.

CLOGGER. Aye, sir.

CHAS, AUDREY, CEM *and* NICKY *gather round, away from* RUDI.

CHAS. What are we gonna do?

CEM. Are you not listening? He's a Nazi. Put a bullet between his eyes.

CHAS *shakes his head*.

It's the only way to be safe.

NICKY. He doesn't look that dangerous.

AUDREY. I thought they were supposed to be blond.

And big.

NICKY. And dressed in shiny black boots.

AUDREY. He looks like a tramp.

NICKY. A really stinky tramp.

AUDREY. And he looks hungry. Can I give him a cup of tea?

CEM. No.

NICKY. Give him my cocoa.

CEM. No!

NICKY. It's gone cold.

CEM. No!

CHAS. Go on, let him. What harm can it do?

AUDREY *fetches the cup of cocoa and gives it to* RUDI.

CLOGGER. Hands, er, downer.

RUDI *grabs the cup and drinks it in one.*

AUDREY. Thirsty.

RUDI. More?

CLOGGER *motions for* RUDI *to put his hands back on his head.*

CEM. If we're not going to shoot him, what are we going to do with him?

AUDREY. Take him to Mr Liddell at the warden's post.

CHAS. What, with a loaded Luger stuck in his back? That'll spark a few questions. Besides, he'll tell them about us.

AUDREY. But he can't speak English.

CLOGGER. I bet he can. Speak English, can't ye?

RUDI. *Klein.* Little.

CHAS. Anyway, they'll interrogate him in German.

CEM. Errol Flynn did that.

CHAS. And then he'll split about this place and the machine gun and then we've had it.

NICKY. So what are we going to do?

RUDI *collapses and falls on his side.*

CLOGGER. Hey!

CEM. He's dead.

NICKY. Is he dead?

CHAS *and* AUDREY *rush to* RUDI. CHAS *feels his pulse.*

CHAS. Asleep. Fainted.

AUDREY. I don't think he's very well. He's shivering.

CHAS. Help us shift him, then tie him up.

The gang lift him up and sit him upright.

AUDREY. Nazis are bloody heavy.

CEM. Oh no, he's gonna die on us. He's gonna die. We're gonna have a Fortress with a dead Nazi. And he's gonna smell just like the one in the plane. He is, isn't he?

CHAS (*simultaneous*). Cem?!

AUDREY (*simultaneous*). Cem?!

ALL. Shut up!

* * *

The McGill kitchen.

RADIO....the Ministry of Defence has today denied speculation that a build-up of German troops in the southern Netherlands is evidence of an imminent invasion. Prime Minister Winston Churchill said British forces were more than prepared for any attempt at a coastal landing along the south coast.

JACK *is looking out the window, shining his shoes.*

JACK (*to the radio*). Prepared along the south coast? What about the north, eh? Do we not matter up here?

He turns the radio off.

(*To* MAGGIE, *off.*) Where's that lad of ours then, eh?

If you want me speaking to him you should have him here. I'm late for me post again.

MAGGIE *enters holding two plates of egg and chips. She sets one down for* CHAS *and one for her. She sits and eats.*

It's not usual he misses his tea?

MAGGIE. Last few weeks it is. Like I've told you a million times now. He's out all day. If I do see him, it's sneaking in the back gate, a wild look in his eyes.

God knows what he's up to.

JACK. It'll be nothing, pet.

MAGGIE. Then why was that policeman round this morning. And yesterday?

Asking question after question about where he was.

The shame of it when I didn't know.

And he parks his bike outside the house each time. The neighbours, Jack.

I want it stopped. Promise, before you go, you'll tell him. He's to stay home from now on.

JACK. Aye.

MAGGIE. Will yer? All week you've said yer will. And all I hear from yer now is 'aye, aye, aye'.

JACK. Hinny, am I not working all hours?

MAGGIE. So am I! In this house!

JACK. You know, it's not just Chas running wild. The whole country's unravelling. At night, I'm at me post and it's not Germans I'm fighting but my own people. Stopping them looting, thieving, fighting.

Enter CHAS.

MAGGIE. I can't do it all on me own. I'm so tired.

JACK *and* MAGGIE *stop suddenly.*

CHAS. What?

MAGGIE. Dad's got something to say to yer. Go on, Dad.

JACK *clicks his fingers and points to a chair at the table*.

JACK. Where've you been?

CHAS. Fishing.

JACK. Fishing?

CHAS. Aye.

JACK *and* MAGGIE *share a look*.

MAGGIE. Yer rod's upstairs.

CHAS. I've used Cem's.

What?

MAGGIE. We've had the police round again. The constable says he's seen you going over to the harbour.

CHAS. He's been following me? Dad!

MAGGIE. And he wanted to know if you'd seen that Mrs Nichol's son.

CHAS. Nicky? He's dead.

MAGGIE. The constable reckons he's alive and hiding out in a camp somewhere with some Scottish boy.

And that missing machine gun.

MAGGIE *places* CHAS*'s dinner in front of him*.

He thinks you're involved.

JACK. So what do you know?

CHAS. Nowt.

JACK *pulls the plate away from* CHAS.

JACK. You're not lying to me?

CHAS. No.

JACK. Cos yer don't lie to me, do yer, son?

CHAS. No… no, Dad.

JACK. I don't want to find out you are. And yer mother doesn't want any more visits from that idiot Hardy.

Say, 'I have not got that machine gun.'

CHAS. I haven't got any machine gun.

JACK *considers* CHAS *then pushes his plate back to him.*

JACK. I want yer home by four each day. So we know where yer are.

CHAS. Dad! That's not fair.

JACK. It's for yer safety. Says in the paper the tide's high. Ya knar what that means?

CHAS *shakes his head.*

Perfect for the Germans' flat-bottomed boats to get over our beach defences. If Hitler's gathering his troops in Holland and Belgium, that means he's preparing an invasion.

If the tide's high it could be any day – by the end of the week maybe.

CHAS. Germans in Garmouth!

JACK. By the end of the week.

* * *

The Fortress.

RUDI *sleeps on one of the bunk beds. He twists, groaning. He is watched attentively by* NICKY, *holding the pistol.*

Enter CEM, *eating from a tin of corned beef.*

CEM. No change?

NICKY. No. He's still making really strange noises.

And he's sweating something chronic.

RUDI *coughs violently in his sleep.*

CEM. Think he's as poorly as he's making out?

NICKY. Aye, I think he's got bronchitis.

Maybe we should get a doctor, Cem.

CEM. But Chas said we're to contact nobody.

NICKY. I know but –

CEM. If we get found out –

NICKY. But if he dies. What will we do then?

Go and get a doctor, Cem.

CEM. If I get a doctor, he'll sprag on us. And you'll go into a home.

NICKY. I know but –

At least he'll still be –

Oh God.

I don't know.

Where's Chas?

CEM. I'll get him some water.

Exit CEM, *leaving the tin of corned beef behind.*

NICKY *approaches* RUDI. *He takes a hanky out of his pocket and wipes* RUDI*'s forehead.*

RUDI *wakes suddenly.*

RUDI. *Mein Gott, wo bin ich?*

NICKY *jumps backwards. He points the gun at* RUDI.

Bitte, bitte. Mein Freund. Pistole.

RUDI *indicates that* NICKY *should lower the gun.* NICKY *shakes his head.*

Ja!

(*Makes gunshot noise*.) Me dead.

RUDI *holds his hand out for the gun.*

Hier. Pistole.

NICKY. But then you'll shoot me and run away.

RUDI. Run? Me?

RUDI *coughs.*

Nein.

RUDI *weighs* NICKY *up.*

(*Pointing to himself.*) Rudi.

NICKY *nods.*

NICKY. Rudi.

Nicky.

RUDI. Nicky.

RUDI *holds out his hand to shake.*

Mein Freund?

NICKY. Friend?

NICKY *doesn't shake* RUDI*'s hand.*

RUDI. *Ja.* Nicky, I want *wasser.* Water?

NICKY. Cem. Cem's getting you water.

RUDI *coughs and splutters.*

RUDI. Who are you? Not soldiers. Like Hitler Youth?

NICKY. No, just kids. Kids from Garmouth.

RUDI. So this is a game, yes?

NICKY. No. This is no game. This is Fortress Caparetto. We're
watching out for Nazis like you. Stop you invading our
country.

RUDI. I am no Nazi.

NICKY. You're German. That makes you a Nazi.

RUDI. No. It is different. I am pilot. I fly in the plane and I fire the gun in back. I do not like Nazi.

NICKY. You're just saying that. I'm not stupid. I've seen the films. Nazis say anything to make people trust them. Then they stick a knife in their back when they're not looking.

RUDI. No, not me. I promise.

What is you do when Nazi soldiers come here?

NICKY. Whatever it takes. This is our home, my home. You lot won't take it off us.

RUDI *motions towards the tin of corned beef.*

RUDI. Please, Nicky.

NICKY *shakes his head.*

I am hungry, very hungry.

NICKY. Suppose you could have a bit. Won't hurt.

You're not allowed to tell them that I'm… you know.

NICKY *approaches* RUDI *gingerly. He feeds* RUDI *corned beef on a fork.*

Now swallow it.

It's just corned beef. It's good for you.

RUDI *pulls a face and swallows. He grimaces.* NICKY *offers* RUDI *more.* RUDI *shakes his head.*

I thought you said you were hungry.

RUDI. Maybe not so hungry. You English eat this beef?

NICKY. Please yourself.

It's not beef. It's 'corned beef'.

This is a 'tin' and this is a 'spoon'.

RUDI *coughs, then coughs again violently.*

I'll get you some of Chas's mother's cough mixture.

NICKY *puts down the tin, leaving the Luger unattended. As*
NICKY *looks for the cough mixture,* RUDI *gets one hand*
free and stretches over for the gun. He grabs it. But decides
against it and puts it back. NICKY *finds the cough mixture.*
And turns. RUDI *puts his hand back in the binding.*

Got it!

NICKY *spoons cough mixture into* RUDI*'s mouth.* RUDI
swallows. NICKY *puts the cap back on the bottle and*
returns it to the shelf. As he does...

This'll make you better.

RUDI. Thank you.

Nicky, you are good kid, yes?

I can see you are good. In your eyes.

Will you – ?

NICKY *turns.* RUDI *holds out his tied hands.*

NICKY. You need to go to the bog?

RUDI. Bog, no.

Free, hands.

NICKY *shakes his head.*

NICKY. I can't.

RUDI. Please.

NICKY....

RUDI. I want to be free. I do not like being tied up like an
animal.

You know I will not escape. Why would I? You feed me this
tin beef, I sleep, I get well again.

You are good friend to me. Better than friends I have in
Germany.

In a prison camp I would be cold, hungry, with no friends.

I have only you.

You know I will not harm you.

I know you will not shoot me.

Bitte.

RUDI *holds his tied hands out.* NICKY *looks around. He unties* RUDI.

See?

I give you my word that I will not harm you or anyone.

Enter CHAS, CLOGGER, AUDREY *and* CEM.

CHAS. Hey, what's he doing?

CLOGGER *grabs the gun.*

CLOGGER. Hands up, Fritz!

RUDI *puts his hands up.*

NICKY. No, wait!

CLOGGER. You untied him? What ye doing?

CHAS. He's supposed to be tied up.

NICKY. He won't hurt us.

CLOGGER. He said that, did he?

RUDI. *Ja.* I am your friend.

AUDREY. He is.

CEM. God, Nicky, yer chockhead, he's a Nazi.

RUDI. No, I am pilot. Only pilot.

NICKY. And he's all right. I've been teaching him English.

RUDI. I read *Dandy.* Is good.

CEM. He's still a Nazi.

    Yer can't trust him.

NICKY. You can, Chas. He's not like the others.

RUDI. I can help you.

CLOGGER. How?

RUDI. Your Fortress. If there is invasion soon, it must be
stronger. You need defences, wire –

CHAS. That's what I've been thinking.

CEM. Yeah but –

Enter AUDREY.

RUDI. Then let me help you.

CHAS. Why not make him work. It's in the Geneva Convention.

CEM. Yer cannet make a prisoner of war help you against his
own people.

CHAS. Yer can if it's not war-work. I know a farmer who's got
two Italians milking his cows.

CLOGGER. I dunno.

CHAS. This place needs to be like Fort Knox.

AUDREY. Aye, Fort Knox with a proper bog.

CHAS. We don't need a bog!

AUDREY. We do too. It's starting to stink out there.

CEM. I don't care.

AUDREY. No, cos it's all right for youse. You're not a woman.

CEM. And you are?

RUDI. Hey, I will make it. With you.

The gang look to each other. Then to CHAS.

CEM. Chas?

CHAS. No. There's something else yer can do.

You were a rear gunner, right?

RUDI. *Ja.*

CHAS. Then you must be pretty handy with a machine gun.
You'll know how to fix one.

CEM. Aye.

RUDI. No, it is too dangerous for little –

CLOGGER. Little what?

CHAS. If yer don't, we'll shoot yer.

RUDI. I plead the Geneva Convention. Prisoners of war are never shot.

AUDREY. That's right. You cannet shoot him!

CEM. We could hand yer over to the Army.

RUDI. But so many questions they would ask. I might the beans spill.

CHAS. We do need the gun fixed.

Don't we?

CLOGGER. Aye. It's got to be fixed.

CHAS. We wouldn't fire it. Except at –

We wouldn't fire it. Just have it… as a mascot.

RUDI *thinks*.

RUDI. I do you a deal. I cannot here be when there invasion is. I will a traitor be, yes.

You get me a boat so I can sail back to Germany. Then I will fix your gun.

CHAS. Vote.

They all put their hands up. Except CEM. CHAS *kicks* CEM *and he then puts his hand up.*

Deal. Sergeant Rudi Gerlath, you're now a temporary member of Fortress Caparetto.

NICKY *smiles at* RUDI. RUDI *looks down at* NICKY, *slightly uncomfortable.*

* * *

A path through the wood. Dusk.

CHAS (*T/A*). So here I am, on my tod, running zigzags along
the cliffs and harbour, looking onto jetties and into sheds.

Someone round here must have a boat.

A boat they could lend us.

Cos the tides are high.

And high tides mean only one thing: invasion.

CHAS *stops. And listens.*

What's that? A crack of a twig snap.

Nothing.

No one.

I'm starting to hear things.

BODDSER *drops out of a tree, a pair of binoculars around
his neck.*

BODDSER. Where you going, McGill?

CHAS. Boddser. What do you want?

BODDSER. I've been enjoying a spot of birdwatching, McGill.

Yer'd like this.

There're some interesting nests built round the Nichol house.

Very nice.

The birds are a lot bigger than you'd expect. And a lot uglier.

I guess they must like it there.

Quiet. Secluded.

Just the right sort of place to, er, I don't know… hide a
machine gun.

CHAS. Sod off, Boddser, you're not welcome round here.

BODDSER *pushes* CHAS.

BODDSER. Where's the gun, McGill?

CHAS. I haven't got it.

BODDSER. You have so.

BODDSER *pushes* CHAS.

Where's the gun?

CHAS. I. Haven't. Got. It.

BODDSER. You. Have. So.

BODDSER *grabs* CHAS*'s arm in a lock and pushes him, face down, to the floor.*

You're not so tough without your pals or a fist of gravel.

CHAS. Ow.

BODDSER. Aye, have a good scream.

Cos no one can hear yer.

BODDSER *twists* CHAS*'s arm tighter.*

Where's the gun?

CHAS. I. Haven't. Got. It.

BODDSER *adjusts his position and pushes* CHAS*'s head over the edge of the stream.*

BODDSER. Let's see if a quick dunking helps you remember.

BODDSER *thrusts* CHAS*'s head underwater.*

Where is it?

BODDSER *pulls* CHAS*'s head up.*

CHAS. I haven't… (*Chokes.*)

BODDSER. Come on, McGill. You're starting to bore me.

BODDSER *thrusts* CHAS*'s head underwater.* CHAS *flops – playing dead.*

Where is…

McGill? McGill?

BODDSER *steps off* CHAS. CHAS *comes back to life*.

You sneaking cheat, McGill. We're gonna have this out whether you like it or not.

CHAS. Clogger! Clogger!

BODDSER. No point calling for him, McGill. He's in Jockoland.

CHAS. Clogger!

BODDSER. Ah, forget the machine gun. This is just about me and you now. A fight to the death.

BODDSER *kicks* CHAS *in the stomach*. CHAS *howls in pain*. CLOGGER *appears*.

CLOGGER. You been torturing my mate?

BODDSER. No... hey... what are yer –

You're supposed to be in Glasgow.

CLOGGER. And you're supposed to have learnt your lesson.

You started the first fight, picking on weans smaller than you. And you got a beating.

Now you're starting another. And fighting dirty.

Just like the Germans.

BODDSER. He fought dirty last time!

Enter CEM, NICKY *and* AUDREY.

CLOGGER. You've spent your whole life playing dirty.

Ye gonna stop?

BODDSER *lashes out a fist at* CLOGGER... CLOGGER *dodges it*.

Time to play fair, Boddser.

BODDSER *lashes out again*. CLOGGER *ducks*.

What do ye say, Chas, dae I do him proper?

CHAS. It's up to him.

Ya knar where we are now, Boddser. Ya knar about our camp, about Clogger and about the gun.

Yer want to leave us be?

BODDSER. They'll send you away to Borstal, all of you.

CHAS. If you tell them.

BODDSER. Try and stop me!

CLOGGER *looks to* CHAS *who nods.*

CHAS. Do him proper.

CLOGGER *then punches* BODDSER *in the stomach. He doubles up.* CLOGGER *then punches him again. He falls to the ground.* CLOGGER *kicks* BODDSER *in the ribs, hard. As* CLOGGER *hits* BODDSER, *the gang support* CLOGGER. *The fight freezes.* CHAS *narrates:*

Clogger does him proper

Fingers fist

He punches

Shoves his shoulder

Boddser stumbles

Jab on the jaw

Dig in the ribs

Clogger punches

Silent, steady

Fist like a piston

He punches, punches

Kicks, kicks

Stamps

Stamps

Stamps

Stamps –

As the fight becomes more violent, more one-sided, CHAS
and the gang move away, shocked.

CLOGGER *leans over* BODDSER.

CLOGGER. You can put me in Borstal. But you cannae keep
me there. If ye tell, I'll get out, and when I do, I'll come
looking for ye. And I'll finish off what I started today. I'll
kill ye even if I have to hang for it. Ye understand me?

BODDSER *nods*.

CHAS. Enough now, Clogger. He's learnt.

CLOGGER. Away with ye.

Exit BODDSER. CHAS *looks at* CLOGGER, *who is
panting*.

CHAS. Clogger –

CLOGGER. What?

Too much for you, wasn't it.

Guess you'll no' be speaking to me any more, eh. Too much
of a Glasgae hooligan.

You can go to the police if you like.

CHAS....

CLOGGER. It was you who said 'dae him proper'.

CHAS. I didn't know what proper meant.

CLOGGER. Aye, that much you've just learnt then.

Nobody breaks up this gang. And I mean nobody. Not
Boddser, not the police, not your folks and definitely not the
Germans. This is our territory and I will fight to the death for
this place. Aye?

CHAS....

NICKY. Me too.

AUDREY. Yeah, me too.

CEM. And me.

CLOGGER. Chas.

CHAS. Yeah. To the death.

* * *

The Fortress.

NICKY *has been collecting firewood. He starts breaking the sticks, then sits, staring out to sea.* RUDI *enters and notices, and sits next to him.* NICKY *raises his eyebrows but says nothing.*

RUDI. What are you looking at?

No reply.

The sea is quite boring, no?

NICKY. My dad's out there. Somewhere.

I used to come here and wonder which wave he was under.

I still don't – [know]

RUDI. I miss my father too. And all my family. I think, 'What are they doing now, at this minute?' Is my mother stirring soup? My father waiting for the factory bell to ring so he can go home?

Maybe.

I don't know.

I do know, it is very hard to be strong when you feel alone. Even harder when you are so young.

I think you, Nicky, you are strong.

NICKY. I don't feel it.

RUDI. I say same for all of you. You are not like any kids I know. You argue, yes, but you are so… I don't know… tough, grown-up.

It is like they don't have other family either.

NICKY. Dunno why you care.

RUDI. What?

NICKY. I said I don't know why you care. I mean, you'll be leaving here soon anyway.

NICKY *snaps a bigger stick in two with his foot*.

RUDI. I do, Nicky.

But you know I must go home.

I am German. I want to go back to Germany.

I cannot live in the Fortress for ever.

You know that, don't you?

NICKY. But why now?

RUDI. It is not safe here. When the invasion happens, I will be seen as a traitor. And shot like a traitor.

Understand?

NICKY. –

RUDI *picks up the sticks and puts them in a bundle*.

Don't. Go, I mean.

RUDI *looks at* NICKY. NICKY *drops his eyes*.

RUDI. Maybe the deal won't happen. Maybe Chas will not find a boat. And I will not mend the gun.

NICKY (*uncertain*). Yeah.

Exit RUDI. NICKY *looks out to sea. Enter* CEM. NICKY *notices him*.

What? Why are you staring at me?

CEM. Yer must have one.

NICKY. One what?

CEM. A boat. Yer dad was a sea captain and yer must have gone sailing with him before the war.

NICKY. I didn't.

NICKY *walks towards the Fortress, where the rest of the gang are.*

CEM. Yer did! I swear I saw yer out with him once. It was a small boat with a red sail.

NICKY. He hired that from a fisherman.

CEM. Bet he didn't!

All the posh folk have a boathouse on the river. With their butlers and cucumber sandwiches.

CHAS. Yer had a boathouse?

NICKY. Yeah but… it got bombed.

CLOGGER. What about the boat?

NICKY. He didn't have a boat.

AUDREY. Yer don't have a boathouse if yer don't have a boat.

CEM. Where is it, Nicky?

CHAS. Come on, we know you've got one.

They all stare at NICKY.

NICKY. All right all right, it's still there.

CHAS. Where?

CLOGGER. Nicky, come on. What's wrong with you, eh?

Are you part of this gang or no'?

NICKY *hangs his head. Enter* RUDI.

NICKY. But it's my father's.

CLOGGER. Ach, c'mon, man. I'm laying down everything for you. If we're not all in this gang together, then none of us is.

If you're no' gonna stand by me, then I'll pack my bags for Glasgow.

CHAS. Nicky, we've got to give Rudi that boat. Otherwise he won't mend the gun.

CLOGGER. We need the gun.

AUDREY. It's Friday.

CHAS. And Sunday's high tide. Dad said the Germans will come when the tides are highest.

CLOGGER. Ye know what that means?

CEM. We've only got two days.

NICKY. But we'll be fine. We've got the Garmouth Home Guard.

CLOGGER. Think they'll protect ye?

NICKY. Yes.

CHAS. They're eighty old codgers. I've seen them training in Deerden Park. Most of them cannet breathe, let alone fight.

CLOGGER. And you seen their weapons? Rifles from 1890-something. A drainpipe that fires rockets… sometimes! And their tank! An old car wi' a wooden turret stuck on top.

CHAS. They're a con. Just a trick to make housewives feel safe in their bed.

We're the only ones who can save this town.

NICKY *takes the key from around his neck and gives it to* CHAS.

NICKY. It's at Priors Haven. You'll need this for the padlock.

CHAS. Come on, you show me and Audrey where the boat is.

Rudi, we're getting you that boat. Now you've got to mend the gun.

RUDI. I don't know if –

CHAS. Yer promised. It's a deal. An honest deal.

CEM. So will yer?

NICKY. Will you, Rudi?

RUDI *nods reluctantly.*

CHAS. Let's get moving.

We're running out of time.

* * *

The McGill kitchen.

An air raid begins. The sound of sirens whining and dogs barking.

CHAS (*T/A*). We were running out of time. Cos the next night, Saturday night

Five o'clock on a Saturday night

I'm at home

And the sirens start screaming early

Too early, a day early, a day before they're supposed to. Me mam and dad run in the kitchen.

Blacking out all the lights

I put down me plate and look out the window

All the lights in Marston Street turn to black

But not the sky, the sky lights up

Beams of searchlights cross the sky like a swordfight.

Dad getting his uniform

Mam pretending everything's all right

And me, at the window, waiting, waiting for the fire show.

JACK *and* MAGGIE *enter.* CHAS *joins them.*

JACK. This could be it, hinny.

Planes first to soften us up, then the boats will come with tanks and / the troops.

MAGGIE. You don't know that, Jack. Not for sure. No one's said they're invading tonight.

JACK. The tide's up, pet. I'm sure it's tonight.

They'll take the harbour in minutes.

Then march on the town, overwhelm the Home Guard, then push on, take the Police Station, Town Hall, the barracks at Blyth. Panzer tanks will be swarming over Garmouth before dawn.

JACK *grabs his warden's hat and jacket.*

MAGGIE. Jack, what are you doing?

You're going out?

JACK. Aye, to the post.

MAGGIE. What about us?

JACK. Stay in the shelter, hinny. I'll look after meself.

What?

C'mon, Maggie, Garmouth needs us!

MAGGIE. We need you!

Jack, are you –

The sound of bombers flying overhead. A distant explosion. MAGGIE *jumps in fright.*

CHAS. Where was that?

JACK. Over by Monkseaton, I'd say.

Bombs are getting closer. I've got to go.

MAGGIE. But, Jack…?

MAGGIE stops.

…when they come, they'll shoot you. I can't… I don't want to…

MAGGIE kisses JACK hard on the lips.

Don't –

JACK. Look after your mother, son. Don't get hit.

JACK exits.

* * *

FATTY *walks down Marston Street with his gas mask on. He lifts it up to blow his whistle.*

FATTY. Get to your shelters!

Everybody into your shelters.

* * *

The warden's post.

A small room in Garmouth High School, with tables with telephones on them, and chairs. FIRST WARDEN *sits, taking incoming calls.*

JACK *enters and is approached immediately by* LIDDELL, *in warden's uniform, who hands him a paper report.*

LIDDELL. Where have you been?

Ashington's been hit; Glebe Street's gone.

A Heinkel's knocked out a barrage balloon and it's crashed onto a farm at Hawthorn.

JACK *takes the report from* LIDDELL *and reads.*

FIRST WARDEN (*shouts*). There's fifty men trapped by a bomb down the Rising Sun Colliery.

LIDDELL (*to* JACK). Area HQ are on to that.

JACK *picks up a telephone and sits*. FIRST WARDEN *answers a call*.

(*To* JACK.) But they need to know about the farm at Hawthorn.

JACK (*to* LIDDELL). Any word on the harbour?

LIDDELL (*to* JACK). No word.

JACK (*to* LIDDELL). Nothing? No boats?

FIRST WARDEN *finishes the call. He holds up a report card*.

LIDDELL (*to* JACK). Nothing.

FIRST WARDEN (*to* LIDDELL). South Shields gas holder's been hit and it's burning, / three men trapped.

LIDDELL *takes the report card and gives it to* JACK.

LIDDELL (*to* JACK). Tell HQ about that too.

Fire engines are needed, remember.

Exit LIDDELL. *Enter* SECOND WARDEN, *holding a report card. He gives it to* JACK.

FIRST WARDEN (*to* JACK). McGill, what did yer say about the harbour?

SECOND WARDEN (*to* JACK). Infirmary's on fire, two wards hit by incendiaries and spreading.

JACK (*to* SECOND WARDEN). On fire?

FIRST WARDEN (*to* JACK). What about the harbour?

McGill.

JACK *dials out*.

JACK (*to* FIRST WARDEN). I don't / know –

SECOND WARDEN (*to* JACK). Two wards have been hit. There's a widespread evacuation. Tell Area HQ / that –

Enter LIDDELL *carrying a report card. He gives it to*
SECOND WARDEN *who sits behind* FIRST WARDEN.

LIDDELL (*to* FIRST WARDEN, *interrupting*). Bomb's hit the
baker's in Greg Street.

She picks up the phone and dials out.

SECOND WARDEN (*to* LIDELL). Infirmary's on fire.

LIDDELL (*to* JACK). Area HQ know about the farm at
Hawthorn?

JACK (*to* LIDELL). Yes, sir.

LIDDELL (*to* SECOND WARDEN). There's a barrage balloon
down on Boyne Street near the harbour.

SECOND WARDEN (*into mouthpiece*). Yes, baker's in Greg
Street. It's on fire.

FIRST WARDEN (*to* LIDDELL). What was that about the
harbour?

SECOND WARDEN (*into mouthpiece, louder*). It's on fire.

LIDDELL (*to* FIRST WARDEN). Yes, Boyne Street in the
harbour.

FIRST WARDEN (*to all*). Fire in the harbour?

SECOND WARDEN (*to* FIRST WARDEN). Is there? Where?

LIDDELL (*to* SECOND WARDEN). Barrage balloon is down
and burning.

SECOND WARDEN (*into mouthpiece*). Bombs, of course
German.

JACK (*to* LIDDELL). Where?

LIDDELL (*to* JACK). In the harbour.

JACK (*to* LIDDELL). What about Germans?

FIRST WARDEN (*to* JACK). Where?

LIDDELL (*to* JACK). No boats or Germans.

JACK (*into mouthpiece*). Yes, at Hawthorn.

(*To* FIRST WARDEN.) Germans?

FIRST WARDEN (*to* JACK). In the harbour.

SECOND WARDEN (*to* FIRST WARDEN). What about Germans?

JACK (*to* SECOND WARDEN). They'll land in the harbour.

FIRST WARDEN (*to* LIDDELL). Have they landed?

SECOND WARDEN (*to JM*). In the harbour?

JACK. Are there Germans in the harbour?

SECOND WARDEN. There are?

> *Both* FIRST WARDEN, JACK *and* SECOND WARDEN *pick up their phones and speak into them.*

FIRST WARDEN. Unconfirmed reports of enemy landing.

SECOND WARDEN. Germans in the harbour.

JACK. Germans have landed in the harbour.

* * *

The McGill shelter.

CHAS *sits turning a model Spitfire over and over in his hands, making a rat-a-tat noise in time with the gunfire above him.*

A flustered MAGGIE *holds her knitting in her hand.*

MAGGIE. Chas, the neighbours…

They're saying… there's Germans in the harbour.

MAGGIE *listens again.*

…Landed on lowboats.

They'll be marching in towards the high street.

With their guns and their grenades.

What are we going to do, Chas?

MAGGIE *freezes*.

CHAS. I don't know, Mam –

I don't…

A muted 'pfff' of an explosion, a Spitfire flies in the distance… then… the distant peal of church bells. They get gradually louder.

MAGGIE. Listen.

CHAS. I can't hear anything, Mam.

MAGGIE. No, no, listen.

The church bells get louder.

There. Church bells.

CHAS *looks to* MAGGIE. *She looks back worried. They know what this means.*

CHAS. Maybe someone's getting married.

MAGGIE. It's coming up from Blyth way. I'm sure there's plenty of soldiers in Blyth.

CHAS. Then it's true. It's the Germans. They've landed.

* * *

A jetty at Priors Haven. Evening.

RUDI *and* NICKY *are by the shore.* RUDI *has a backpack by his feet and two oars in his hands.*

NICKY. Remember, use your oars till you get clear of the Castle Cliff. And then pull on the red rope to raise the big sail. You won't need the little sail so don't worry about the blue rope.

RUDI. Okay.

RUDI *picks up his rucksack.*

I think that is all.

NICKY. You've got enough food?

RUDI. Oh yes. Audrey was very kind. I will miss lots of things about your country. But the corned beef? No.

NICKY. Rudi?

RUDI. *Ja?*

NICKY. Can I come with you?

RUDI. To Germany, no.

NICKY. I could sail the boat for you. I'm an expert, honest.

If you go and the boat goes then there's nothing left.

RUDI. *Nein*, you have much left. Your *Kameraden*. They are good kids.

NICKY. But I like you better.

Better than I liked my old dad.

RUDI. And I like you better than any of my family.

NICKY. So?

RUDI *kneels next to* NICKY.

RUDI. I am sorry.

NICKY. You don't care. You don't care what happens to us.

RUDI. I do.

NICKY. If you did, you wouldn't leave.

RUDI. I will see you after the war, Nicky. When we will all be *Kameraden*.

NICKY *nods*.

Promise me one thing, Nicky.

Never fight.

No wars are noble or right.

Nobody wins them. One side just loses less.

Use your life for something worthwhile.

Not all this.

RUDI *steps into the boat.* NICKY *offers* RUDI *his hand to shake. They shake.*

NICKY. Bye, Rudi.

RUDI. Goodbye, Nicky.

* * *

Midnight. Amid the sound of explosions and sirens, the children are escaping.

CHAS (*T/A*). 'Mam, Mam, I need the lav,' I says, 'I've got to go. Now, Mam, before the Germans come.'

'No,' she says.

'But I've got to go!'

'Okay then, go,' she says.

So I step out the shelter, towards the house, towards the lav and…

CEM (*T/A*). 'We're going to the graveyard,' Dad says.

'The cemetery?' Mam says.

'Why?' I says.

'Because it's safer,' he says. 'We'll go down into the Irving Tomb. The doors is best bronze and the walls is two foot thick.'

'But it's full of dead folk,' Mam says.

'And haunted,' I says.

'S'all right, Dad says, 'I've taken out the bodies and coffins. The Germans will never find us underground.'

AUDREY (*T/A*). 'Daddy, where are we going?' I scream on the back seat

Of the car as it screams through the back streets.

'We're going to your Auntie Emily's in Westmoreland,' he says.

'In the country.'

'But Churchill said we're to stay put!'

'Churchill? Damn him to hell,' says Daddy. 'He's probably on a plane to Canada with the Royal bloody Family.'

'Are we running away, Daddy, are we cowards, Daddy?

Are we running away?'

CHAS (*T/A*). I'm running out the back gate, down the back alley

Running away, away from my house

The dark lanes, bombs and fires

Past Peach Street, Rose Street

Over the fields and through the woods.

CEM (*T/A*). Sprinting now, away from the cries and shouts of me mam and dad

Past the gravestones, dodging past the tombs and bodies

Out the gates, onto the high street, to the sea and to / the –

AUDREY (*T/A*). The car stops, I push the handle, the door swings open

And I'm out the car, foot down, hit the road

And I'm running, blind and in a panic.

Pitch black but I know where I'm going.

CHAS (*T/A*). To the Fortress –

CEM (*T/A*). To the Fortress –

AUDREY (*T/A*). To the Fortress.

* * *

The Fortress.

As CHAS *speaks, the gang prepare the Fortress for combat.*

CLOGGER *is in the crow's nest with the telescope and the Fortress Caparetto tin hat, looking out to sea.* AUDREY *sits near him with a pen and paper, jotting down the locations of boats.* CEM *unwraps the machine gun, which is wrapped in one of Captain Nichol's old shirts.* NICKY *sets up the tripod. They set the tripod and gun.*

CHAS *stands looking out to sea.*

CHAS (*T/A*). At the Fortress, we're ready and waiting, surveying the sea.

Defences built and bolstered

Posts manned and camouflaged

Weapons to hand

As the hours tick by

And night turns into morning

We keep our concentration

This is it now; our chance to save Garmouth.

CLOGGER. Captain! Forty-nine north by north-east. Two ships: minesweepers.

Three degrees east. A lookout drifter –

CLOGGER *turns ten or twenty degrees, scanning the horizon.*

Twenty-three north by north-north-east. Unidentified vessel progressing south-westerly.

AUDREY. Identify, Petty Officer.

Is it an enemy vessel?

Can you confirm? Yes or no?

CLOGGER *looks closely.*

CLOGGER. Unable to identify.

CHAS. Assume yes, Quartermaster.

Keep an eye on it.

And across the heath, Private, any sign of troops approaching?

NICKY. Nothing yet, sir.

CHAS. The Germans should be here by now. It's getting light.

CHAS *turns his attention to* CEM *and* NICKY.

Update on the weapon, Sergeant Jones?

CEM. Fully operational, sir. We're ready and waiting.

CHAS. Good.

The enemy could emerge from any direction and hit land any moment.

CHAS *looks out to sea.* AUDREY *folds her book.*

AUDREY. Captain, I've been thinking, if we fire on them, sir, then they'll, if they've got guns too then...

CHAS. Then what?

AUDREY. You know...

CHAS. We'll just have to make sure we hit them before they hit us.

AUDREY. If we don't – ?

CHAS. –

Any more on the vessel, Petty Officer?

CLOGGER. No, it's still heading towards South Shields, sir.

AUDREY *hasn't moved*.

AUDREY. Captain – ?

CHAS. We're gonna be all right.

You've been a top-quality quartermaster.

And Cem, he's been a great sergeant, Nicky the best private, Clogger a champion petty officer.

AUDREY. Aye and you've been all right too, Chas McGill. I thought you was stupid with all your daft plans but now maybe I think… aye well… you're not too bad.

A whistle in the distance. They stop.

CEM. What was that?

NICKY. A whistle. Came from the heath, sir.

CHAS. The heath?

Petty Officer? Eyes on the heath, now.

CLOGGER *turns and looks with the telescope*.

AUDREY. What can you see?

CLOGGER. Cannae tell. It's too misty…

CHAS. Friend or foe?

CLOGGER. Ach, they're… there's tonnes of them, dozens.

AUDREY. Jerry?

CLOGGER. There's uniforms, I'm… I dunno… aye, they're coming this way.

CHAS. Let me.

CLOGGER. They're up to the white fence.

NICKY. That's two hundred yards!

CLOGGER *throws the telescope to* CHAS *who looks*.

CEM. Are they Jerry, Captain?

CHAS. Can't tell. The mist. Hang on… erm… Fatty Hardy's with them.

CLOGGER. He must be a traitor.

CEM. A defector?

CEM *crouches behind the gun.*

NICKY. Maybe he's their prisoner.

CHAS. Doesn't matter.

CLOGGER. They look like Jerry, sir.

CHAS. Company, ready!

Sergeant Jones, prepare the defence.

CLOGGER. One hundred and fifty yards approaching.

CEM. Wait. What's the time?

CLOGGER. Forget about the time, man.

CEM. Audrey?

AUDREY. 6:27 exactly.

CEM. And it's near light. There's no way the Germans would invade now, not in the morning.

CHAS. We don't know that. Sergeant, assume the position to fire.

CLOGGER. Eighty yards. Stay focused, company.

CEM *stands, away from the gun.*

CHAS. Come on, Jones. All you've wanted to do is fire the gun. Now's your chance. Now get in position and prepare to fire.

CEM. But, sir, we don't know it's Jerry.

CHAS. We can't take the risk, Jones.

We fire now or we're all dead.

CEM *shakes his head.* CHAS *jumps behind the gun and aims.*

Well?

CLOGGER. I say we fire.

AUDREY. Fire!

CLOGGER. Seventy yards, sir.

NICKY. Fire!

CEM. Wait. Don't. Yer can't fire without knowing!

AUDREY. Come on, Chas. We can't take the chance.

CLOGGER. Fifty yards, sir.

CHAS. Too late, Sergeant.

Preparing to fire.

CEM. No Chas, please!

CHAS. Ready. Aim. And fire!

CHAS *fires the gun. It roars, smoking.*

* * *

The sound of return gunfire.

* * *

The gang duck the gunfire and run for cover behind the sandbags.

CLOGGER. They're firing back!

CHAS. It is Jerry.

CLOGGER. Fire again!

CHAS *fires the machine gun.*

* * *

Enter RUDI, *dishevelled, tired and cold, holding a white flag on a twig.*

* * *

The Fortress. The children are still hiding behind the sandbags.

AUDREY. They've stopped firing!

CEM. Why have they stopped firing?

CLOGGER. You must have got 'em, man!

CHAS. Did I?

Did I get 'em?

CLOGGER *jumps up to a vantage point with the telescope.*

AUDREY. I can't see anything!

CHAS. What can yer see, Clogger?

CLOGGER. Rudi.

NICKY. Rudi's come back?

CLOGGER. Aye, talking to Fatty Hardy.

CEM. I knew it. He must have led them to us. I knew we couldn't trust him.

CLOGGER. Aye, he's pointing over here.

Stan Liddell's with them too.

CHAS. He's a traitor too?

AUDREY. Is that… is that me mam?

CLOGGER. And your mam too, Cem. She looks really angry.

CEM. They're all traitors.

CLOGGER. Och.

CHAS. What?

CLOGGER. Chassy, your daddy's there too.

CHAS. Oh.

CHAS *is knocked for six.* RUDI *begins approaching the fortress.*

He's not a –

He wouldn't –

He can't be.

CEM. The Germans must be using them as hostages.

AUDREY. I can't see any Germans.

Just lots and lots of the Home Guard.

And our mams and dads.

CLOGGER. They're coming this way.

AUDREY. What we gonna do? They can't all be traitors.

CHAS. Arm yourselves.

CEM. But they're our parents.

CHAS. Not any more they're not.

They all look to CHAS. *They pick up their weapons –* CHAS
picks up the machine gun, CLOGGER *the Luger pistol,*
AUDREY *and* CEM *pick up sticks and bricks.*

AUDREY. They're nearly –

Oh God, they're coming, Chas.

CEM. Oh no, what have we done?

CHAS *climbs on top of the Fortress.* RUDI *is now close by.*

CHAS. Go back, sod off. Leave us alone. If you don't, we'll
shoot.

AUDREY. Go away!

CEM. Leave us alone! This is ours.

CHAS. Sod off! This is ours.

RUDI. Chas! Don't shoot!

I am your friend.

CHAS. Get back, Rudi!

Or I'll shoot, I will.

RUDI. It's all over! There is no invasion. There are no soldiers.
No Germans. Only your families.

*CLOGGER climbs down from the tree. He points the Luger
at RUDI.*

CHAS. We don't care!

CLOGGER. They're no' taking this from us even if it's over my
dead body.

He turns his head away and fires.

*The bullet hits RUDI square on the shoulder, knocking him
down.*

CEM. No!

Rudi!

AUDREY. Rudi!

NICKY. Rudi!

CHAS. You've hit him.

Our friend, Clogger.

*The children put down their weapons and crowd around
RUDI.*

AUDREY. Is he all right?

NICKY. Is he alive?

CEM. Are you, man, are you all right?

Oh no, Chas, look at him.

What have we done?

* * *

*The gang dismantle the Fortress and then, finally, the
machine gun.*

CHAS (*T/A*). The ambulance took Rudi away to hospital.

I gave up the gun to Mr Liddell.

Fatty Hardy took the Luger.

And the Home Guard took over the Fortress.

All our mams and dads blamed each other.

There was lots of shaking heads and talk of punishment.

None of them understood us

Or knew why we'd done what we done

All except me dad that is.

Voice of JACK.

JACK. I can't say there was sense in all that, lad, but I'll say this. When some people panicked and others tried to run away, you stayed and fought. And that took guts. Real guts.

CHAS *nods. He watches as* AUDREY, CLOGGER, NICKY *and* CEM *finish dismantling the machine gun and prepare to leave the Fortress. As* CHAS *speaks, they exit.*

CHAS (*T/A*). Audrey spent the rest of the war at her auntie's in Westmoreland. Her mam put her in an all girls' school full of ladies who were brought up proper. Try as she might, though, Audrey's mam never did get her into wearing hats and pretty dresses.

Cem was dragged home, given a bucket and sponge and made to scrub every gravestone in Garmouth Graveyard. He did them all without complaining once. Aye, well maybe just once.

Nicky was fostered by a family in Whitby who were all right. He sent us postcards every month with news about him learning to sail his dad's old boat.

Clogger was put on the train back to Glasgow. But never arrived. He jumped off at Edinburgh and signed up with the Army, saying he was eighteen. Until the war ended, he was fighting in France, for his country.

Me, I picked up a handful of spent cartridges and went back to me house at nineteen Marston Street. I missed me mates and I missed the adventure. Mam didn't speak to us for a week and Dad made me return all the things we'd pinched. I might have done meself no favours. But would I change a single thing we'd done? Never.

Fortress Caparetto!

End.

www.nickhernbooks.co.uk

facebook.com/nickhernbooks

twitter.com/nickhernbooks

ROBERT WESTALL

Robert Atkinson Westall was born in North Shields,
Northumberland, on 7 October 1929. He wrote his first book,
The Machine Gunners, drawing on his own childhood
experiences during World War II, to be read aloud to his son,
Christopher. It was published in 1975 and went on to win the
Carnegie Medal in Literature. He won the Smarties Prize and
the Guardian Award as well as a second Carnegie Medal for his
1981 book *The Scarecrows*. His books have been translated into
many languages and dramatised for television. *The Machine
Gunners* was named as one of the top-ten Medal-winning works
for the seventieth-anniversary celebration for the Carnegie
Medal in 2007. He died in 1993.

ALI TAYLOR

Ali Taylor's other plays include *Sticks and Stones* (Polka
Theatre); *A Little Neck* (Goat & Monkey, Hampton Court
Palace); *Overspill* (Soho Theatre/Churchill Theatre, Bromley);
59 Cups (Topos Allou, Athens); *Cotton Wool* (Theatre503,
winner of the eighteenth Meyer Whitworth Award); *Porcelain*
(Royal Court Jerwood Theatre Upstairs, Workers Writes
Festival) and *Hive9* (Islington Community Theatre). For BBC
Radio 4, he has written *Cinders* and *Eight Feet High and
Rising*. Ali is an artistic director of Buckle for Dust theatre
company (www.bucklefordust.org.uk).

Other Adaptations in this Series

ANIMAL FARM
Ian Wooldridge
Adapted from George Orwell

ANNA KARENINA
Helen Edmundson
Adapted from Leo Tolstoy

ARABIAN NIGHTS
Dominic Cooke

THE CANTERBURY TALES
Mike Poulton
Adapted from Geoffrey Chaucer

A CHRISTMAS CAROL
Karen Louise Hebden
Adapted from Charles Dickens

CORAM BOY
Helen Edmundson
Adapted from Jamila Gavin

DAVID COPPERFIELD
Alastair Cording
Adapted from Charles Dickens

DR JEKYLL AND MR HYDE
David Edgar
Adapted from Robert Louis Stevenson

DRACULA
Liz Lochhead
Adapted from Bram Stoker

EMMA
Martin Millar and Doon MacKichan
Adapted from Jane Austen

FAR FROM THE MADDING CROWD
Mark Healy
Adapted from Thomas Hardy

FRANKENSTEIN
Patrick Sandford
Adapted from Mary Shelley

GREAT EXPECTATIONS
Nick Ormerod and Declan Donnellan
Adapted from Charles Dickens

THE HAUNTING
Hugh Janes
Adapted from Charles Dickens

HIS DARK MATERIALS
Nicholas Wright
Adapted from Philip Pullman

THE HOUND OF THE
BASKERVILLES
Steven Canny & John Nicholson
Adapted from Arthur Conan Doyle

JANE EYRE
Polly Teale
Adapted from Charlotte Brontë

THE JUNGLE BOOK
Stuart Paterson
Adapted from Rudyard Kipling

KENSUKE'S KINGDOM
Stuart Paterson
Adapted from Michael Morpurgo

KES
Lawrence Till
Adapted from Barry Hines

MADAME BOVARY
Fay Weldon
Adapted from Gustave Flaubert

NOUGHTS & CROSSES
Dominic Cooke
Adapted from Malorie Blackman

PERSUASION
Mark Healy
Adapted from Jane Austen

THE RAGGED TROUSERED
PHILANTHROPISTS
Howard Brenton
Adapted from Robert Tressell

THE RAILWAY CHILDREN
Mike Kenny
Adapted from E. Nesbit

SENSE AND SENSIBILITY
Mark Healy
Adapted from Jane Austen

SWALLOWS AND AMAZONS
Helen Edmundson and Neil Hannon
Adapted from Arthur Ransome

TREASURE ISLAND
Stuart Paterson
Adapted from Robert Louis Stevenson

WAR AND PEACE
Helen Edmundson
Adapted from Leo Tolstoy